Street Woman

In the series

Women in the Political Economy,
edited by Ronnie J. Steinberg

Street Woman

Eleanor M. Miller

TEMPLE UNIVERSITY PRESS
Philadelphia

Library of Congress Cataloging-in-Publication Data

Miller, Eleanor M., 1948–
  Street woman.

  (Women in the political economy)
  Bibliography: p.
  Includes index.
  1. Female offenders—Wisconsin—Milwaukee.
  2. Prostitution—Wisconsin—Milwaukee.   I. Title.
  II. Series.
  HV6046.M47   1986   364.3'74'0977595   85-26133
  ISBN0-87722-417-X

The paper used in this publication meets the minimum requirements
of American National Standard for Information Sciences—Permanence
of Paper for Printed Library Materials, ANSI Z39.48-1984.

Temple University Press, Philadelphia 19122
© 1986 by Temple University. All rights reserved
Published 1986
Printed in the United States of America

To Dale

Contents

Acknowledgments

There are many people who have had some role in giving me the particular sociological perspective I brought to this study and the concrete methodological and analytical skills necessary to do it. The person to whom I owe the largest debt for the former is Donald N. Levine, Professor of Sociology and now Dean of the College at the University of Chicago. Without having encountered this inspiring teacher who gave me so much by way of social and emotional support, I would certainly not be a sociologist today. For the latter I must heartily thank Gerald Suttles, Professor of Sociology at that university as well.

There are also those to whom I owe thanks for initially stimulating an intellectual interest in those who are stigmatized and treated inhumanely because of their race, ethnicity, sex, or socio-economic status. Among them are Marie Augusta Neal of Emmanuel College, Charles Lidz of the University of Pittsburgh, and William Julius Wilson of the University of Chicago.

Among those whom I have on occasion cursed, but have mightily appreciated most of the time, are those who gave me a haunting feeling of personal responsibility to those we sociologists speak of so clinically as the underclass. These include my father, Thomas J. Miller, who has always had such a keen eye for injustice; the women of the Sisters of Notre Dame de Namur who were my teachers and the first and most important role models of academic womanhood I really ever had; and, more currently, fellow members of Sociologists for Women in Society too numerous to mention who share my concerns and are ever supportive of research such as is described here.

Whatever inspiration, knowledge, and skill are evidenced in the pages of this book should very much be credited to those I've mentioned above, then; whatever ignorance, error, or lack of understanding or empathy remains I claim as my own.

The people at Temple University Press were helpful at all stages of the preparation of the manuscript. Especially for his enthusiasm about this work from the very outset, I would like to thank Editor-in-Chief Michael Ames.

There is one area where I have accrued a large debt that I have yet to mention. Those who have given me intellectual, technical, social, emotional, and other sorts of invaluable support are many. I would like to thank Laurel Richardson, William Kornblum, Cecilia Ridgeway, Donald Noel, William Chambliss, Ronnie Steinberg, Gerald Suttles, Morris Janowitz, and William Julius Wilson for reading and commenting on the entire manuscript. I would also like to thank the Department of Sociology at the University of Wisconsin–Milwaukee for the many and varied ways in which its members were helpful, especially Jane Hood, Joan Moore, William Mayrl, and Ronald Edari. Friends and fellow-travelers who much deserve a word of thanks for always being there when needed are Lois McDermott, Marianne Steele, and Joseph Catania. The Irene E. Miller Foundation should be gratefully acknowledged for financial support at a crucial stage of the fieldwork. For their patient and careful technical assistance, I would like to express my appreciation to Diane Eisold, Irene Miller, Deborah Richie Kolberg, Zona Selensky, Billy Crawford, and Gerald Graczkowski. A special word of thanks is also due cartographer Donna Schenström, who adapted maps originally prepared by Frances Beverstock for my use. Mrs. Beverstock kindly gave me permission to use her work and her contribution to this book thus deserves acknowledgment as well.

Without the efficient and dedicated staffs of Wisconsin Correctional Services, the Department of Corrections of the State of Wisconsin, Arc House, Horizon House, and Metro Center, it would not have been possible for me to have gained access to the population of women I was interested in coming to know. Janice

Brylow of WCS deserves particular thanks. She not only opened jail cells but organizational doors as well. Attorney Allen Eisenberg was also of help to me in this regard. An enormous debt is obviously owed those women themselves. They spoke openly with me about some very painful and private areas of their lives. They were generous in the extreme. It is my sincere hope that this book helps them and the growing numbers of women like them and does them no harm.

When I offer words of gratitude to by husband, Dale Jaffe, only he really knows how much I owe him. For toilets scrubbed, diapers changed, gourmet and inedible meals prepared, I love him dearly. For his unstinting faith in my ability to do this study and the sacrifices he made in his own work and personal life so that I might, I am forever in his debt. For the many times this, the sociologist always best able to critique my work, read the words that follow and reassured me that what I was saying was important to say, I am sincerely appreciative. For his continuous and unsuccessful efforts to get me to be more organized, I thank him as well; they will provide us with stories to laugh about together for years to come. And, because there is much that is too private to thank him for here, I dedicate this book to him.

Street Woman

CHAPTER
I

The Sociological Study of the Criminality of Women

For a long time, the social sciences were silent on the topic of the criminality of women. It was a silence that lasted a quarter of a century, from the publication of Otto Pollak's *The Criminality of Women* in 1950 to the appearance in 1975 of Freda Adler's *Sisters in Crime* and Rita James Simon's *Women and Crime*. The particular thematic interpretations advanced by Adler and Simon instantly captured the interest of the media and stimulated their colleagues to attempt to specify further or refute their findings. Their efforts were pathbreaking, then, and for that reason they are important. That their original theorizing may have led much of the interested public as well as some of their colleagues down an intellectual dead-end street, however, has only recently become apparent.

Both works elaborate a theme that links increases in the criminality of women in the United States since the late 1960s to the contemporary "women's movement." Simon attributes a dramatic rise in crimes against property committed by women to an *objective* change in the circumstances of women made possible by the women's movement: recent increases in their labor force participation. Adler, on the other hand, attributes what she sees as a general increase in the criminality of women to a *subjective* change: recent shifts in sex role attitudes and orientations. Both explanations have been shown to have serious flaws and this fact is an impetus for the advancement of alternative explanations.

3

At the outset, it is important to note that there is little disagreement at this point about the fact that selected property offenses have been on the rise among women (Mukherjee and Fitzgerald 1981; Steffensmeier 1980). Those popular exposés, such as Adler's, designed to show the increasing violence of women inevitably do so by comparing the percentage increase in crimes against persons for which women have been arrested with those for men. The exceedingly low base rates for women for these sorts of crimes make very small absolute increases into very large percentage increases. It is this sort of statistical distortion that leads Adler to conclude that, with the exception of murder and aggravated assault, the picture of female arrest rates' rising faster than male arrest rates is a consistent one across the board (see Miller 1983 for a more detailed discussion of these methodological issues).

Those who feel, like Simon, that women's increased labor force participation explains the rise in their property offense rate argue that it is the accompanying increased opportunities to commit embezzlement, forgery, fraud, and other white-collar crimes that are crucial.[1] There are several problems with this sort of explanation. First, available data indicate that the women who have entered the labor force in recent years have, for the most part, taken jobs that have typically been "women's jobs." They are service workers, clerks, typists, salespeople (Gross 1968; U.S. Department of Commerce 1970). In short, women are not in positions where they can commit serious property crimes in the course of their work to a much greater degree than they were in the past. Furthermore, there is evidence that what appear to be serious white-collar crimes are, in reality, often petty street crimes. For example, the increases in fraud referred to above are often instances of credit card fraud, the increases in larceny instances of shoplifting; forgeries are often engaged in by signing others' names to stolen personal checks, which are cashed for petty amounts. The data provided to criminologists by the FBI's *Uniform Crime Reports (UCR)* just do not differentiate very well between the one

---

1. In a parallel sort of analysis, Simon (1977) argues that the reason the female crime rate in Israel has not increased since 1960 is that the proportion of women who work outside the home on a full-time basis has not increased since that time. It is her feeling that the absence of a significant women's movement in Israel is an important link in the explanatory chain.

sort of fraud, larceny, and forgery and other, more serious, sorts. Neither are dollar amounts specified for embezzlement (Steffensmeier 1980). Second, the greatest rise in property offenses among females seems to be concentrated among those women who, because of their youth, have little or no acquaintance with the world of work (Noblit and Burcart 1976)

The second explanation, that favored by Adler, links the rise in female offenses to attitudinal changes associated with the women's movement. It assumes that the ideas of women as well as their behaviors are coming more and more to resemble those of men. If this were so, one would expect a rise in the violent offenses committed by women to parallel the rise in property crimes. As mentioned above, this has not occurred. In addition, although the FBI data indicate 1966–1967 as the point at which the rates for selected property crimes begin and continue to increase, other research indicates that the change in women's sex role attitudes toward a more egalitarian stance has been rather gradual and that, in fact, most American women were not even exposed to the contemporary women's movement until the *end* of the 1960s or the early 1970s (Mason, Czajka, and Arber 1976).[2]

The reason that Adler and Simon could interpret the *UCR* data as they did is not simply because the use of inappropriate descriptive statistics misled them or because a lack of knowledge about which sorts of crimes might be subsumed under which FBI categories clouded their reasoning. It is additionally, I would argue, because they were out of touch with who the typical female criminal in this country is on both a demographic and a personal level.

Even with proper caveats regarding the possible biasing effects of differential treatment by race and class as women progress through the stages of the criminal justice system that lead from arrest to incarceration, available demographic data on women who have, in recent years, been in prisons and jails combined with data on women who have been on probation and parole offer a strikingly consistent portrait of the female criminal. Historically, and especially at present, she is young and poor and

2. Another interesting piece of evidence is Morris's study (1973) of coverage received by the women's movement in Los Angeles County. It reveals that neither of the two major newspapers there provided much information on the movement until after 1970.

belongs to a minority. She has limited education and skills, is the mother of several children, and has been involved in prostitution, a petty property crime, or a drug offense (Chapman 1980: 60).

A 1976 study of these women by the U.S. General Accounting Office (1979) indicates that seven out of every ten women imprisoned for felonies at that time were first arrested for prostitution. The most widespread of female offenses, however, were property offenses. Nearly 25 percent of all arrested women were apprehended for larceny, as compared to only 8 percent of all men arrested. Fraud accounted for 6 percent of female arrests, 2 percent of male arrests. Moreover, while women made up only 11 percent of arrests for violent crimes, they accounted for 38 percent of arrests for fraud, 36 percent of embezzlements, and 35 percent of larcenies. More black women committed larceny than any other property crime. Forgery and fraud along with drug violations were the most common crimes among white and Native American women. For Hispanic women, drug violations were by far the major crime. Lastly, recidivism among female property offenders was very high (17-19). The authors of this report answered their own rhetorical question concerning the motivation of these women by observing: "Well, clearly these property crimes have an economic object. They are a source of ready cash, and as such they meet the very real needs of the typical female offender, who is generally poor" (19).

Who she is in a more personal sense and just how she came to be involved in the activities described above, however, are very much mysteries. The research undertaken as the basis of this work seeks to begin to answer these and related questions because they are important and interesting in and of themselves, but also so that future efforts to theorize about changes in the criminality of women in the aggregate may be a bit better grounded in reality.

The work at hand is a study of female street hustlers who were living and engaging in illegal work, especially prostitution, fraud, forgery, embezzlement, and larceny, in Milwaukee, Wisconsin, in 1979.[3] It is based primarily upon information gleaned

---

3. The definition of "hustling" employed here is that of Bettylou Valentine. It refers to a wide variety of "unconventional, sometimes extralegal or illegal activities, often frowned upon by the wider community but widely accepted and practiced in the slums" (1978: 23). The focus here is exclusively on that part of hustling that is illegal.

from topical life history interviews completed with a sample of these women during that year. One cannot assume that all of the women described demographically above were street hustlers. However, on simply the level of common sense, two pieces of evidence are important. First, even if the biasing effect of the sifting and winnowing that occurs by race/ethnicity and class as women travel through the various stages of the criminal justice system is very great, one would expect, if the crimes being committed in increasing numbers are white-collar crimes, to see these white-collar criminals appearing in increasing numbers in prison/jail census studies, like the one discussed above. This has not occurred. Second, if the GAO study is accurate and a substantial number of women in prison and jail and on probation and parole have prostitution as their first offense, does it make sense to think that a woman is likely to engage early on in her life in selling sex for money and only later advances to embezzlement and fraud committed in the context of a white-collar job? I think not.

Furthermore, the trends in female criminality since the late 1960s noted nationally are very much mirrored in the trends for Wisconsin female offenders among whom Milwaukee women are disproportionately represented (Table 1). For reasons that will become obvious as we examine the details of their lives, it is probably safe to assume that the flesh-and-blood women who make up the data for Wisconsin, too, are primarily female street hustlers.

Obviously, qualitative research of the sort employed in this study cannot "test" macro-level correlations of the type proposed by Adler and Simon. What it can do, however, is to offer descriptions and analyses of actual women of the kind being theorized about in the aggregate. Ideally, we should be able at least to recognize the individual in the picture painted of the group. It should not be too much to ask that research at the macro level not fly in the face of in-depth studies of the everyday experiences of the individuals being aggregated. Moreover, such grounded research should itself yield middle-range theory that helps bridge the gap between individual behavior and macro trends by suggesting some of the mechanisms by which the one gets translated into the other.

To this end, the topical life history interviews completed in Milwaukee were analyzed to try to get a sense of how the social

TABLE 1
Female Crime as a Percentage of All Reported Crime in Wisconsin, 1969-1976

Offense	Year							
	1969	1970	1971	1972	1973	1974	1975	1976
Murder	14	15	21	14	14	6	18	13
Robbery	7	5	4	5	6	7	7	8
Aggravated assault	12	10	13	11	10	11	10	12
Burglary	3	4	5	4	3	4	5	5
Larceny/theft	25	28	29	31	29	28	27	30
Motor vehicle theft	5	5	6	6	6	7	8	8
Prostitution and commercialized vice*	95	87	94	84	85	77	86	85
Embezzlement†	5	28	22	10	15	22	0	45
Forgery	22	23	25	27	31	27	28	33
Fraud	28	30	31	32	34	33	33	35
All crime index offenses	17	20	21	22	21	20	19	21

SOURCE: *Wisconsin Crime and Arrests* (Madison: Crime Information Bureau, Department of Justice, 1969-1976), as cited in Bowker (1978).

* The fact that these percentages do not increase may reflect the fact that an increasing number of males may now be subject to arrest for these offenses. The overwhelming majority of arrests in this category, however, are of females.

† When working with very small numbers of cases, a greater amount of statistical variability between years will be found than when working with large numbers of cases.

8

world within which these young women lived and grew shaped their participation in illegal work. From there, one can better hypothesize, I would argue, about how that social world itself is molded by structural and cultural changes at the macro level.

Hustling as Underclass Work

In his book, *The Underclass* (1982), Ken Auletta has described a sample of underclass men and women who are in the process of trying to acquire the social and technical skills that will supposedly make them employable. He highlights the episodic character of their lives with regard to straight living and work, welfare receipt, hustling, and intermittent personal family crisis. The culture of the underclass, that set of ideas and beliefs that characterize the group, is also the focus of Auletta's attempt to account for the difficulties these people have in adjusting to work in the straight world.

The title of Auletta's fine book is a bit misleading. Although he does present a cross-section of underclass persons, and they do vary in age, race, and sex, they are all presented at a particular juncture of their lives, the point at which they are attempting to enter the world of "legitimate" work. He is only observing, in the setting of the job-training office, those persons who make such an attempt. I would argue that before one can speak in any global way about the contemporary underclass, however, one needs many more such cross-sections. The current work, then, may be seen as complementing Auletta's. It is one more step in the direction of what should be a cumulative effort on the part of social scientists to describe and analyze a whole.

The cross-section presented here focuses on those underclass women from their mid to late teens to their late twenties or early thirties who hustle a living on the streets of a moderate-sized midwestern city: Milwaukee, Wisconsin. The majority of the women studied are black. Many of them come from households that have for generations lived in poverty and, at least for the last several generations, received some sort of public welfare assistance. These are not the only women so engaged, however. The underclass has, by definition, certain caste-like characteristics. There is some limited mobility for its membership such that people do move up and out of this class, but these people are not the focus of the current study. Those female street hustlers whose families are not clearly from the underclass are females moving in the opposite direction. They are downwardly mobile women from working-class and middle-class families whose children will very likely be solidly underclass. These women, too, are described in the pages that follow. While many of them are also minority women, they are much more likely to be white. Their children may be of mixed race and are likely, because of the prejudicial basis upon which race is assigned in our society, to be identified as black and to grow up completely identified with the minority that dominates the ranks of the underclass. Although the original impetus for this work was my interest in the debate surrounding recent increases in the property crime rates for women, then, once in the field I realized that here was a world that social scientists knew little about that was of interest in and of itself.

Technically, almost every instance of hustling engaged in by these women is legally definable as a crime. Representatives of the criminal justice system with whom these underclass women have frequent interactions have no trouble defining their behavior in this way. Looked at from the point of view of the women themselves, however, hustling is *work* that someone who has not shared their precarious lives has defined as in violation of the law. This is not to imply that they themselves do not, in large measure, share those definitions. It is, however, to suggest that hustling for them is simply "illegal work" that underclass people often engage in just as upper-class people spend their time doctoring and lawyering. It is what many underclass people do at one time or another to make ends meet; it is what these particular women do most of the time during this particular period of their lives for economic reasons as well as for reasons that stem only indirectly from economic deprivation. After listening to a number of them, I too soon began to see hustling as work and, thus, have chosen to speak of it as such here.[4]

The research presented in the pages to follow, then, does not pretend to shed light on the world of the underclass as a whole or

---

4. The view of hustling as "work" may go a long way in accounting for the reluctance of the underclass people Auletta (1982) studied to pursue training for "straight" jobs. In a very real sense, these people already have work experience to the degree that they have been involved in hustling. Of course, hustling has its price, but from the point of view of the underclass hustler, so does "straight" work.

even on the world of the female underclass as a whole. My lens is not a wide-angle one; my focus is very limited. This work describes and analyzes in some detail a certain portion of the lives of one segment of the female underclass, those young women who are recruited to street hustling and engage in this illegal work, generally to the exclusion of straight work, for a substantial period of their lives. It is, I hope, a significant addition to our cumulative knowledge of the lives of underclass people generally, but most especially it provides certain insights into the lives of the young women who are its specific subject. In addition, it contributes, I believe, to a broader understanding of those structural, economic, and cultural conditions that are crucial to interpreting the criminality of women. Lastly, the work has certain implicit ramifications for public policy and explicit implications for further research.

Milwaukee and Its People

All of the fieldwork for this study of female street hustlers and the majority of the interviews on which it is based took place in the city of Milwaukee, Wisconsin. For the most part, the women who are the subject of the study were born in that city, went to school there, hustled there, and were arrested there.

Milwaukee is located on the shores of Lake Michigan, about ninety miles north-northwest of Chicago. The city itself makes up a substantial portion of the county in which it is located, Milwaukee County (see Map 1, where the city boundaries have been accentuated in bold outline). At the time of the study, 1978–1979, the city was the sixteenth most populous city in the nation. It had an estimated population of 637,317 (Wisconsin Department of Industry 1979: 1). Milwaukee is known as the city made famous by its beer, but it was also a leader in industrial production and a major food-processing center. Because such a large portion of its economic life revolves around the production of heavy machinery and foodstuffs, it is a city of skilled and semi-skilled laborers with a decidedly blue-collar flavor (Cianciara 1978: 44–59).

Like many other northern cities of its kind (for example, Pittsburgh), it is now in many ways a city in decline. Due to prolonged recession, the availability of cheaper, more easily dis-

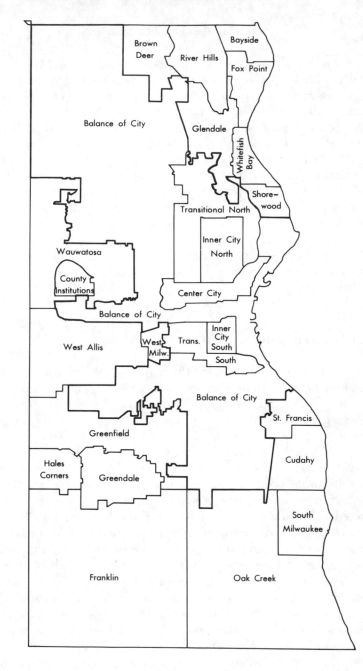

MAP 1
Milwaukee County Area

ciplined labor elsewhere, foreign competition, and an outmoded physical and technical infrastructure, it has been plagued by runaway shops. Thus, its large force of skilled and semi-skilled laborers have suffered from high levels of unemployment as, of course, have its unskilled workers and service workers.

The Racial and Ethnic Composition of the Population

There were 1,447,900 people living in the Milwaukee Standard Metropolitan Statistical Area (SMSA) in 1976 (Edari 1978: 86). A breakdown of this population according to "racial" categories is shown in Table 2. This table shows that, of the people living in the Milwaukee SMSA in 1976, 10.7 percent were members of nonwhite minority groups. Blacks were the largest minority group (8.2%), followed by Hispanics (1.8%), Native Americans (.3%), and Asians (.2%). The 1975 Special Census indicates that

TABLE 2

The Racial Composition of the Population of the Milwaukee SMSA, 1976

	Number	Percent
White	1,291,525	89.2
Black	119,180	8.2
Native American	4,850	.3
Asian	3,590	.2
Other races	2,385	.2
Hispanic	26,370	1.8
Total minority	156,375	10.7
Total population	1,447,900	99.9*

SOURCE: Wisconsin Department of Industry, Labor, and Human Relations, *Manpower Information for Affirmative Action Programs: 1976* (Madison Employment Security Division Job Service, 1976), as cited in Edari (1978:88).

* Total does not add up to 100 due to rounding errors.

almost all the members of minority communities lived in the city of Milwaukee, where they comprised 19.2 percent of the population. Of this minority population blacks made up 18.5 percent. It also indicates that the black population is much younger than the white population and that the degree of sex imbalance is greater for blacks than for whites (as cited in Edari 1978: 86–87).

Although the majority of white Milwaukee residents are native-born, there are many foreign-born, and ethnic identification is great. Within the city itself, residential patterns are strongly associated with ethnicity. The largest ethnic groups in the city at present are composed of immigrants and descendents of immigrants from Poland, Germany, Italy, and Ireland. Other countries of ancestry include Sweden, Switzerland, Finland, Russia, Scotland, Belgium, Czechoslovakia, Croatia, Austria, Greece, France, and Lithuania (Tien 1962). Although there have been a number of Puerto Ricans and, especially, Chicano immigrants to the area in recent decades, Hispanics are not new to the city. Chicanos came in substantial numbers to work in the city's tanneries in the early twenties. Recruiters were sent to Mexico, where they persuaded whole villages to come. A large flow of Chicanos from Mexico and the Southwest did not reoccur until after World War II (Gurda and Anderson 1972: 5). The most recent foreign-born immigrants to come in any numbers have been from Southeast Asia.

The Social Ecology of Milwaukee

The neighborhood areas depicted in Map 2 are considered by their inhabitants as well as by other residents of the county to be discrete geographical and social units.[5] Each has a distinctive history and racial and ethnic flavor as well as characteristic geographical features. The city neighborhoods are grouped together by residents in terms of their location vis-à-vis the center city area. These larger areas also have distinctive characteristics in terms of housing stock, residential and business mix, and the racial and

5. The community area representation in Map 2 was devised by Beverstock and Stuckert (1972) and was the result of a cooperative effort on the part of the Department of Sociology at the University of Wisconsin–Milwaukee and the Urban Observatory, which was located at that university, to apply to Milwaukee some of the techniques employed by the Social Science Research Committee of the University of Chicago (1963).

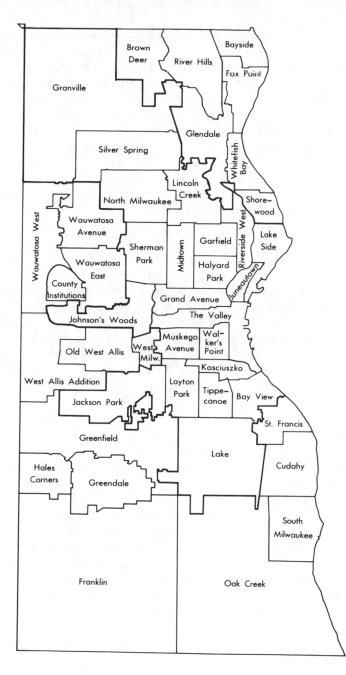

MAP 2
Metropolitan Milwaukee Community Areas

ethnic composition of the populace. They are not neighborhoods in the sense that the smaller units are, however, simply because the residents have little attachment to each other that is rooted in shared geographical area. In relationship to downtown, there is, then, the Eastside (Lake Side), Westside, Northside, and Southside. There is also the Far Westside, Far Northside, and Far Southside. The Northside and Southside have been further divided by city planners and social scientists into areas called Inner (or Center) City North and Inner (or Center) City South, and Transitional North and Transitional South. The inner or center city designation generally denotes an area of the city where the housing stock is very old and, where, for some time, the population has consisted of the elderly, the very poor, and minority members. The transitional designation indicates an area of slightly better housing, an area where the upwardly mobile from center city areas often move and on the periphery of which some gentrification on the part of young, white professionals may have occurred. These areas are generally ones where, over the last two decades, minority members have gradually replaced whites, however, as ethnic whites have moved out of the city and the numbers of blacks, Hispanics, and Native Americans in the city itself have increased.

The worst housing, then, and the greatest number of abandoned units are located in these inner city (center city) areas. They also have, generally speaking, the highest overall crime rates (see Map 3). Inner City North includes the neighborhoods of Halyard Park and Garfield. Transitional North includes the neighborhoods of Midtown, Lincoln Creek, and Riverside West. Sherman Park, the area just west of Midtown, is an integrated area that also appears to be on the decline. Inner City South includes the Valley and Walker's Point (an area undergoing some gentrification). Transitional South includes Kosciuszko and Muskego Avenue. (For these areas see both Maps 1 and 2.) In short, as one goes north of Juneautown and Grand Avenue, the area designated center city (the western portion of which is a fringe area in which residential and business units uneasily coexist with the major downtown area for hustling), and south of downtown (an area that has recently undergone, and continues to undergo, substantial urban renewal and constitutes the easternmost part of center city, extending a bit northward along the Lake), one encounters the city's underclass.

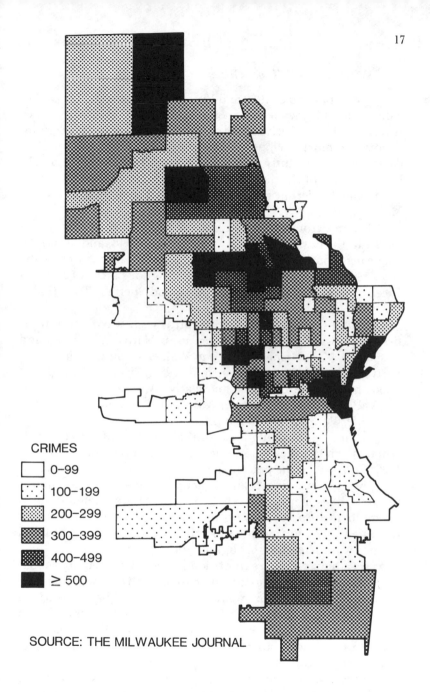

CRIMES

☐ 0–99

∴ 100–199

▦ 200–299

▨ 300–399

▩ 400–499

■ ≥ 500

SOURCE: THE MILWAUKEE JOURNAL

MAP 3
Crime in the City of Milwaukee, 1984

Milwaukee's Two Cities

A comparison of 1970 and 1980 census data lends support to a thesis about Milwaukee that originated in the 1960s: Milwaukee is very much two cities. It is also clear that this thesis is becoming a more and more obvious one over time. On almost any variable, data differ significantly when one compares figures for the neighborhood areas of Garfield, Halyard Park, Midtown, and Walker's Point and bordering areas with other city neighborhoods (see Maps 1 and 2).

Figures from the 1980 census show that 53 percent of all blacks in the city lived in Halyard Park, Garfield, and Midtown. These neighborhoods were each over 90 percent black. Most of the city's remaining blacks lived in the contiguous areas of Lincoln Creek, Grand Avenue, Riverside West, and Sherman Park (Palay 1984: n.p.).

Blacks shared their center city areas with two other minorities in 1980 and during prior censuses: Native Americans and Hispanics. Most Hispanics lived in Walker's Point, to the south. Forty percent of them lived there in 1980. Five other neighborhoods had sizable Hispanic and Native American populations: the Valley, Muskego Avenue, Kosciuszko, Grand Avenue, and Riverside West (Palay 1984: n.p.).

Almost all outlying areas of the city showed very low percentages for families below the poverty line in both 1970 and 1980. Conversely, the percentage of families with incomes below the poverty level increases as neighborhood location moves towards the center of the city. Not surprisingly, neighborhood unemployment patterns were also associated with distance from the center city. During this time, the percentage of unemployed persons was increasing throughout the city. At any point in time, however, the percentages in predominately black neighborhoods were two or more times greater than the overall city percentage. In 1980, when the city figure was 8.9 percent, the figure for Garfield was 17.0 percent, for Halyard Park 16.2 percent, and for Midtown 15.2 percent. Walker's Point, Kosciuszko, Grand Avenue, and Lincoln Creek were all approaching double-digit official rates (Palay 1984: n.p.).

The inner city areas also have the highest levels of single female family heads. About 40 percent of family heads in Halyard Park, Garfield, and Midtown were single women. Percentages become successively lower as areas approach the city's perimeter.

Moreover, data on single female family heads changed considerably between 1970 and 1980, as did other measures of economic well-being. In 1970, the city figure was 10.6 percent. By 1980, it had risen to 15.5 percent. Following national trends, more and more women were becoming heads of households, more of them and their children were falling into the ranks of the poor, and, in Milwaukee, they constituted a larger and larger proportion of center city residents (Palay 1984: n.p.).

Moreover, according to a recent study by the Children's Defense Fund, Milwaukee has the highest percentage of births to black female teenagers among the twenty-seven largest U.S. cities. Statistics compiled by the child advocacy group in 1982 show that 29.7 percent, or 1,175, of births to black women in Milwaukee were to teenagers. Moreover, 93.1 percent of babies born to black adolescents in 1982 were born to unmarried young women. The magnitude of the differential is illustrated by a 1983 Wisconsin Department of Health and Social Services comparison of live births to teens using the Zip Code designations of their home addresses to do an ecological analysis of teen births by city area. The Zip Code area containing most of the city's black neighborhoods recorded 198 births to females seventeen and younger, including 18 to children aged fourteen or younger. In contrast, the Zip Code areas of the predominantly white and higher-income North Shore (the independent villages along the lake, north of the city) recorded only one birth to an adolescent girl (*Milwaukee Journal*, March 27, 1985).

What emerges, then, is a picture of a city highly segregated by race/ethnicity and income. Milwaukee, along with Chicago, Illinois, Gary, Indiana, and several other cities has the dubious distinction of being among the most residentially segregated cities in the country depending upon how that designation is arrived at. In fact, what one sees is, indeed, two cities: a peripheral white city that has certainly fallen victim to the national recession and the erosion of the local economy but, despite that, remains relatively affluent and an increasingly poverty-ridden, predominantly minority inner city.

Female Street Hustlers and Their Neighborhoods

The Inner City North and Transitional North include the neighborhoods where the majority of the nonwhite informants in this study (and since they constitute the largest group in the study, the majority of informants, generally) spent their youths, where their children and their children's caretakers reside, and where they themselves sometimes live and often work. The Hispanics in the study came from Inner City South neighborhoods and from St. Francis, which is further south still. Poor and moderate-income ethnic whites tend to live in the area directly south of downtown, in the regions directly south and southwest of these, and, less frequently, north and northwest of Transitional North. The majority of white women interviewed for the study were from southside neighborhoods. Both white and Hispanic women may have hustled in Inner City North and Transitional North neighborhoods even if they never came to live there. This is particularly likely if they have had children by black men and those children are being cared for by kin in those neighborhoods. It is also likely if their hustling at any time has involved them in the networks of people who deal drugs or are engaged in prostitution-related activity there, although such enterprises are also found in some of their neighborhoods of origin as well.[6] The area directly east of downtown and on up the shore of Lake Michigan is, as described above, a fairly affluent white area. The North Shore villages just outside the city limits in the far northeastern part of the county are the areas of greatest per capita wealth (see Map 2). Such villages are Whitefish Bay, Fox Point, and River Hills. Only one woman who participated in this study was from that part of Milwaukee County. There was only one Native American woman interviewed. She was born in Keshena on a reservation in the northern part of the state.[7]

6. In fact, because of the "Mexican Connection," some of my informants who deal and use heroin tell me that the quality of drugs (and perhaps the quantity, as well) is far superior on the Southside. They theorize that the more general poverty of Northside neighborhoods leads to the dilution of drugs at several points. They also describe being charged for a "works" (drug-shooting paraphernalia) on the Northside when that sort of equipment might be provided free to the south.

7. It is my impression that Native American women are not generally drawn into the hustling activity of the streets with black, white, and Hispanic women. Their criminal activity tends to be much more individualistic. It is, broadly speaking, very much influenced by alcohol use. This is a group about which little is known and the work at hand will, unfortunately, do nothing to fill the void. Unlike the members of those other groups, Native American women also seem much more reticent when it comes to discussing their problems and, especially, their illicit behavior. Thus, even the one woman spoken with for this study provided little by way of useful comparative data.

The Inner City North and Transitional North areas are the most important areas with regard to the study of Milwaukee's female street hustlers, then. It is there that the majority of the women on whose lives this book is based grew up, currently live (at least intermittently), and do a good bit of their hustling. The city has three major hustling areas. One is the downtown area already mentioned. The others are in north center city neighborhoods: 27th Street from Wells Street to State Street and North Avenue from 28th Street to 35th Street. Having major female street hustling areas close by was an important factor for some female street hustlers as they grew to adulthood. It meant that, even if there were no hustlers, male or female, in their own households or among their immediate kin, they were likely to be exposed to hustling as possible work for both men and women at a time when all children are thinking about what they will be when they grow up.

This is not to suggest that the blacks in the neighborhoods that constitute these areas (or the households on a particular block, for that matter) are homogeneous with regard to the major income-generating activities of adults, their lifestyles generally, or the ways in which they raise their children. The same neighborhoods that produce female street hustlers also produce many of the nonwhite college students I teach. A careful observer walking through parts of these neighborhoods will observe a variety of lifestyles in the living. Walking south on 27th Street from Capitol Drive, one sees well-maintained houses with flowerboxes filled with petunias and geraniums and little vegetable plots to the side cheek by jowl with ramshackle houses with dirty children spilling from their broken porches and drunk or high young adults lazing in the doorways. On occasion, one comes upon a small locally owned business: a beauty parlor, a small shop that sells fashionable, if poorly made, women's or children's clothes, a storefront church, a grocery, a tavern (which, in this part of the city, is usually termed "a lounge" by the owner—for example, Leon's Twilight Lounge), a small take-out restaurant, a laundromat. There are also liquor package stores, walk-in health-care providers, currency exchanges, gas stations, and fast-food franchises that are, more than likely, owned by outsiders. City and county social service sites are sometimes quite apparent because they bear signs that clearly designate them as such and sometimes only obvious because their constituents do not blend in well with the rest of the community residents. Many of the halfway houses and drug and alcohol treatment centers run by the city and the county are there, for example. A porchload of scruffy, fiftyish, white men staring off into space on a hot summer's day cues the observer to the fact that this is probably one such site.

Driving through these neighborhoods, one comes across areas that have been made relatively inaccessible to automobile traffic because the people living there want to demarcate and patrol their own blocks, of which they are justifiably proud. Generally speaking, however, one is struck by the fact that these neighborhoods are far dirtier than Milwaukee's non-minority neighborhoods, whose cleanliness tends to impress city visitors. There is also a good deal of street life. Children play in the street; women, toddlers in tow, visit on their porches and in front of their homes; large groups wait for buses; young and middle-aged males hang on corners; and young couples flirt and neck in doorways. In some areas, street walkers openly strut their stuff.

North center city neighborhoods, and most Milwaukee neighborhoods for that matter, are not characterized by the medium- or high-rise apartment buildings of larger cities. Most of the homes are bungalows or, more often, wooden duplexes ("two-flats") with small grassy yards to the side or back. Two rows of these houses, each facing a street, are often located back to back, where they are divided by an alley in which cars are garaged or simply parked and where children play. This scheme accommodates the removal of heavy snow from the streets themselves, where only restricted and seasonal parking is permitted. The alleys constitute important play areas, then; they are also often the scene of predatory crimes, sex, and drug dealing.

Just as it would be inaccurate to describe these areas as physically homogeneous, so would it be inaccurate to describe them as culturally homogeneous, especially with regard to those ideas and beliefs that support or discourage different varieties of unconventional, extralegal, or illegal income-generating activities. Although the majority of the inhabitants of north center city neighborhoods are poor by any standard, many would be characterized by themselves, outsiders, and their neighbors as straight-living.[8] On the other end of the continuum, there are families/households whose membership is so problem-ridden that the group occupies a certain pariah status in the neighborhood. My sense is that the most typical cultural and behavioral pattern is somewhere between these two extremes. The physical and social environment is such that it is almost impossible to isolate oneself from one's more desperate, hustling-immersed neighbors. Moreover, the pressures of poverty push the straight-living in that direction, as well. However, it is possible for whole households or goodly portions of households to live primarily straight lives. Straight living is certainly promoted by the ideologies of the religious groups to which these particular people, especially the older women among them, often belong. My sense is that most of the straight-living poor are not, over time, untouched by the deviance about them, however. They are certainly victims of it when one of their members is directly preyed upon, exploited, or actually drawn into the deviant activity that is all around them or, at the very least, quite nearby.

The nonwhite women interviewed for this study come from both sorts of homes, as well as homes that one might best characterize as between the two. The nature of their families/households of origin influences just how they become involved in the deviant street activity that is all around them and patterns what happens after their initial recruitment. But I am getting ahead of myself; this constitutes the story that will be told in the chapters to follow. The stories of the women who, unlike these, end up facing me as I teach will not be told here, although I do hope that someone will tell that story in the future for it is obviously a significant one. Before describing the lives of the young female street hustlers I came to know, it is important to know a bit about how the study was conducted. This is the topic of the remainder of this chapter.

8. In fact, several block associations have attempted to drive street walkers from their immediate areas. A group calling itself SMASH, Stop Mashing and Sexual Harrassment, organized teams of irked neighborhood women to record the license numbers of cars operated by men who openly propositioned neighborhood women and prostitutes and report that information to the police. The police, in turn, were asked to enforce a seldom-used city ordinance dating to 1910 on "mashing"—accosting, insulting, or following a person of the opposite sex (*Milwaukee Journal*, May 26, 1985).

The Study

The Sample of Women Interviewed

The sample was gathered by starting "snowballs" rolling at four different locations: two halfway houses for female offenders (Horizon House and Arc House), the Milwaukee House of Correction, and Metro Center.[9] The two halfway houses primarily contained women who were on probation but had been ordered by the courts to spend some or all of their time at such facilities. The women at the Milwaukee House of Correction were serving sentences of under two years, had had their probation revoked because of a subsequent offense and were awaiting trial or sentencing, or were awaiting transport to Taycheedah Correctional Institution (TCI, the state correctional facility for women). The largest number were in the first two categories. Many of those who were actually serving time (post-sentencing) went to work every day under a Wisconsin work-release program created by something called the Huber Law. These women were expected to reimburse the state for their room and board out of their earnings. Technically, the women at Metro Center were still serving time at Taycheedah. They had negotiated a contract with the parole board, based on their good conduct at TCI, that allowed them to serve the last several months of their sentences at Metro Center, which is located in the YWCA in downtown Milwaukee. These women were also allowed out of that rather secure facility to work or, accompanied by a chaperone, to attend religious services, Alcoholics Anonymous meetings, or other conventional events.

The use of these institutional sites allowed sampling of groups of women on the streets at various points in their deviant careers. The women at the halfway houses tended to be younger and to have been arrested less often and for less serious offenses

9. "Snowball sampling" is a particularly good way to access a hard-to-reach population. One asks one's informant to refer one to another informant. In my case, this involved a female street hustler's actually calling another woman and vouching for me. The drawbacks of this sampling technique are several. It obviously does not produce a random sample. Thus, one never knows *how* representative of the universe (all of Milwaukee's female street hustlers) one's own sample is or *in what ways* it might not be representative of the universe. The justification for the technique is that, whatever its limitations, without its use the study could probably not have been done at all.

than those at the Milwaukee House of Correction. The women that they referred to me were usually also at similar stages in their careers as street hustlers. The women at the Milwaukee House of Correction were, in turn, less seasoned offenders than the women at Metro Center. About one-third of the women interviewed were in one of these four institutions. The remainder were not institutionalized at the time of the interview.

The only criterion I originally adopted for including a woman in the sample was that she have been convicted of something more serious than prostitution. My reason was that I wanted to study female felons, and prostitution is a misdemeanor in Wisconsin. It soon became clear that almost everyone I interviewed had at least one arrest for prostitution as well. This was true for both property offenders and women who had been arrested for violent crimes. This criterion changed, then, but I deliberately limited the number of women with arrests only for prostitution. I also began with the idea of studying female felons, but not necessarily street hustlers. With only one exception, however, the women I interviewed in these institutions were street hustlers. The one exception was a woman who was clearly a white-collar criminal: a forty-five-year-old black woman who had been convicted of embezzling funds from the social service agency where she worked. She was the only woman I interviewed who claimed not to have done the thing she had been convicted of. That interview was omitted at the time of analysis.

Some other interviews were also omitted. These tended to have been carried out in an institutional setting, which, of course, reduces the proportion of interviews of institutionalized women actually used as the basis of the analytic and theoretical discussions contained here. The reason that these particular interviews were omitted was because, in the institutional setting, the researcher had less control over who was to be interviewed and how. This was especially true at the Milwaukee House of Correction. At every other institutional site, I had an opportunity to speak with the women as a group and explain the nature of the study before I contracted with particular women for interviews. At the House of Correction any woman who was interested in being interviewed was brought to me in the prison chapel. I offered a remuneration of ten dollars to women interviewed. Two of the women who were brought to me were clearly mentally deficient but very interested in earning ten dollars. I felt that both interviews should be completed and the remuneration awarded, but the interviews were of such poor quality that they were omitted from the analysis. Three other poor-quality interviews were caused by the interviewing conditions. The chapel overlooked a basketball court on which the men in the House of Correction took exercise. Three interviews recorded on the afternoon of a particularly raucous game were completely untranscribable and repeat interviews could not be arranged. Out of eighty-four women asked, then, I completed seventy interviews, of which sixty-four (91%) are included in the analysis.

Methods of Procedure

The method primarily employed in this study was the life history method. Seventy women agreed to taped interviews with me during which they shared with me the details of their lives. Very few women asked actually refused to be interviewed. For one reason or another, interviews with many of the fourteen women not spoken with simply could not be arranged. The life histories recorded were not complete life histories, but rather topical life histories. The topics were arrived at after a review of the literature and the completion of five exploratory and rather complete life histories. Special attention was paid to the initiation of these women into street hustling and the development of a career line as a street hustler. The review of the literature introduced a number of topics already mentioned relevant to the debate surrounding whether the contemporary women's movement has had an effect on women generally, and on these women in particular, that would result in their committing more crimes and especially crimes thought to be more appropriate to males. The exploratory interviews served to acquaint me in a general way with the vocabulary of female street hustlers as well as with some of their major concerns.

Although the same broad topics were introduced during each interview, many of my questions changed over time. Initial taped interviews were played again and again after being recorded. Tentative hypotheses and emergent behavior categories arose out of these hours of listening. During subsequent interviews, then, I would introduce questions to test these tentative hypotheses by searching for negative evidence and to bring a greater degree of definition to these emergent categories. These sorts of considerations also influenced the direction of the snowball sampling when I had a choice to make about which of several respondents to speak with. Occasionally, it was possible to reinterview women who had been interviewed at the beginning of the study in the light of my accumulating knowledge and increasing familiarity with the female street hustler's lifestyle and vocabulary. A specific set of demographic data was also collected at the time of the interview and entered on a mimeographed sheet designed for that purpose.

I transcribed the tapes myself. This was mainly because of the degree of jargon employed by the informants, the level of background noise, and the general lack of familiarity on the part of those available to do transcription with the rhythms and vocabulary of Black English. This task took approximately eighteen months to complete whereas the interviews themselves were completed over a span of about six months.

In addition to the interviews completed with female street hustlers themselves, other informal and formal interviews were completed with household members and deviant street network members. If the scheduled interview took place in someone's home or hotel room or a room in the back of the tavern, it would occasionally be interrupted by friends who dropped by. Even when I specifically requested that a woman try to set aside a particular block of time for the interview, this sometimes occurred. Such persons, who often knew about the interview that was in progress, would be asked to return later in the day or evening. More often, people would come by after the interview was completed, when the woman and I were sitting around having coffee, some wine, or a beer. In any event, I would on occasion be asked to "hang out and party" for a while. As I came to know street women better and came to be better known myself, these sorts of social invitations increased. I was asked, for example, to a cookout and softball game. If I had gone to someone's family home, often a mother or grandmother would invite me to have coffee. These occasions were frustrating in terms of uninterrupted interviewing, but they often provided opportunities for group discussions of street hustling and sometimes for setting up other interviews. As a result of these meetings, I learned a good deal about street hustling and was able to arrange two formal interviews with the mothers of female street hustlers. If the setting was one in which street hustling actually occurred, I also on occasion was able to supplement my interview data with observational data.

My snowball technique was not very effective in linking me with women who had withdrawn from street life. I was able to arrange interviews with four retired female street hustlers through a student of mine who had been a street hustler and had served time in Taycheedah. This woman has also been willing to read parts of my analysis and discuss them with me. She has been very helpful in making me aware of my own misperceptions, oversights, and biases. The manuscript was also read by a vice officer on the city police force, who also offered helpful corrective comments.[10] Although the analysis here is primarily based on life histories gathered from female hustlers themselves, then, it is often supplemented and informed by other interviews and discussions and by occasional, and very limited, observations.

Possible Problems of the Study

As mentioned above, to get in touch with the women interviewed for this book I used what is called a snowball sampling technique, where each woman interviewed is asked to refer other women. This is a good method for reaching the members of a group that is difficult to reach for one reason or another—in this case because of their hours, the difference between their social class and, usually, race/ethnicity and mine, and their involvement in illegal activity. Without using such a technique, research such as is described here can often not be done. Snowball sampling is not without drawbacks, however. There is, for example, the problem of what social scientists call external validity. One never knows how representative such a group is of the larger universe of such people. For example, it is possible that the particular network of acquainted female street hustlers I accessed with each of my three snowballs is unique in some way. Since my aim is to be able to make accurate statements about Milwaukee's

---

10. In an effort to assure their anonymity, neither of these people is formally recognized for their contribution to the accuracy of this study in my Acknowledgments. I would like to thank them both here.

female street hustlers generally and not just describe the sixty-four women I interviewed, not knowing whether or not there are any significant differences between the former and the latter groups is problematic. In other words, I may make unknown (and unknowable) errors when I generalize from the sixty-four to the universe of female street hustlers in Milwaukee. There is an even greater chance of error should I try to generalize to an even larger group: female street hustlers in the United States, for example. Generalizations, then, must be made with the utmost caution, but it is just such generalization of which science is made. Research such as this, then, provides generalizations solidly grounded in data that become the source of testable hypotheses for subsequent researchers.

To be a bit more directly responsive to the issue of external validity, I might note the following. Unless there is a large group of female street hustlers who have never "caught cases" (been arrested), there is little reason to believe that the women included in the sample of female hustlers used in this study are very different from most other female street hustlers who have been active for some time in this city. My snowball sampling procedure never resulted in a woman who had not yet caught a case. Most women interviewed reported having had an arrest within the first few months of being on the streets. This may be due to their almost uniform early involvement in prostitution, a fairly visible street activity whether one walks the streets or hustles men out of a tavern or a hotel. Because of the visibility of these women and the relationships that develop between them and the police, it is very unlikely that a street hustler can be on the street for any length of time without detection and arrest. It is possible, of course, that women who limit their involvement in street crime to intermittent prostitution in their own homes or some other private place might go undetected. My impression is that there are some women who operate in this fashion, working straight jobs or living on welfare most of the time. Such women apparently do not have careers as street hustlers, nor do they take street hustling as a major part of their identities. They are not the focus of this study and would appear to represent a separate phenomenon. It is my firm belief, therefore, that the study has few problems that derive from a lack of external validity.

There is another possible problem with the sort of study

undertaken here. It has to do with internal validity: the degree to which the data gathered from the informants were accurate. There is rarely a way to confirm the veracity of information communicated during interviews, and ethical considerations at times prevented me from seeking out confirmation when I thought it might be available. Before each interview, I explained to the informant that I was writing a book on female street hustlers. The woman was asked to sign a statement indicating that the interview was given voluntarily and that she was aware of the nature of the study. In return, I guaranteed her anonymity and paid her ten dollars. This meant that, even though one woman had been referred by another, talking about one to the other was to be avoided. The details of certain women's lives sometimes led me to connect one person with another when these individuals were not even contiguous links in the referral chain. There were occasions when I was quite sure I was eliciting evidence confirming or negating the details of prior interviews, yet did not feel free to pursue this. Fortunately, this sort of information was often communicated during the individual interview or at a later time in a group setting without my eliciting it. In such cases, I felt comfortable asking follow-up questions about the *events* being described. In practice, the street networks are so often intertwined that this kind of verification was quite frequent.

There is also the problem of recall and reinterpretation on the part of those being interviewed, even if they are attempting to be fairly open. Obviously, the accuracy of recall and the amount of distortion due to retroactive reinterpretation is significantly related to the nature of the topic in question. On the one hand, I have a great deal of confidence in the data gathered from women about their involvement in criminal activity. I have every reason to believe that, to the best of their ability, they apparently listed and described their criminal behavior. There are two reasons for this conclusion. First, to the degree that they were formally charged with these crimes, their behavior was a matter of public record and the women knew that. Only in one case did I actually check the record, however. Second, the majority of the women told me about crimes with which they had never been charged and, occasionally, about crimes that had not yet been committed. On the other hand, I have less confidence in reports about emotionally charged subjects, especially relationships with family and lovers, and matters of opinion. I attempted during the course of the interviews, especially when informants were skeptical about confidentiality, to bring the topic up again later in the interview, perhaps in a different form. For example, if a woman said that she felt that street women were foolish to give their money to "their men" and return to them after having been beaten by them, I might attempt to reintroduce this topic when the woman was talking about *her* relationship with *her* "man." Very often, women who had held views like the ones expressed here would act in a directly contrary way. It became obvious to me that, at the very least, there was a clear distinction to be made between words and deeds. Alternately, such probing might elicit a description of the circumstances under which this general norm did not apply, or an admission that this was a topic about which there was, in reality, a good deal of ambivalence.

Another issue that impinges on internal validity has to do with the effect of my growing familiarity with the street scene on the quality of my interactions with women being interviewed and, in turn, on the quality of the data over time. During one of my last interviews, an eighteen-year-old black woman asked, "Hey, you ever been a hooker?" I said, "No." She then responded, "'Cause you sure sound like a hooker." What clearly happened over time was that I developed a street vocabulary and, indeed, often found myself switching into a variant of Black English that was spoken by the majority of the street hustlers regardless of race. This, along with a growing reputation among female street hustlers, improved the quality of the data over time. It may also indicate a problem of overidentification. (See the Afterword for a more personal account of the research experience in which some of these issues are explored in greater detail.)

Ethical Considerations: Protecting My Subjects

In presenting case material in the body of this work, only first names are used and those names are fictitious. Other names mentioned by informants have also been changed. The original list of informant names has been destroyed, making it impossible to connect present findings with particular individuals. Although the original tapes of the interviews are intact, informants' names were not usually mentioned during interviews and when they were, their names and other names were erased. In addition, the signed voluntary consent forms were coded and only those codes appear on the file folders containing copies of each typed transcript.

Milwaukee's Female Street Hustlers: An Overview

As mentioned above, basic demographic data were collected on a separate face-sheet at the time each woman was interviewed. These data were later abstracted to provide an overview of selected characteristics of the sample of women upon whose lives this book is based. Several of the more important of these characteristics are presented in Table 3. It is my hope that the reader will keep them in mind during the opening treatment of the nature and context of female street hustling that introduces Chapter II. Brief as they are, they should provide an important orienting focus until the lives of the women themselves can be sketched in greater detail.

Of the sixty-four women interviewed, thirty-five (55%) were black, twenty-four (38%) were white, four (6%) were Hispanic, and one (2%) was American Indian. The mean age of the women interviewed was 23.38 years: for blacks 23.24, for whites 24.17, and for Hispanics 22.0. The American Indian woman was 19. The sixty-four women had eighty-one children among them, includ-

TABLE 3
Selected Demographic Characteristics of the Sample

	N	Mean Age	Mean Number of Children	Mean Years of Schooling	Mean Duration of Longest Employment (months)
Black	35	23.24	1.29	10.53	7.53
White	24	24.17	1.08	11.08	9.71
Hispanic	4	22.0	2.0	10.50	2.17
American Indian	1	19.0	0	9.0	.17
Sample	64	23.38	1.27	10.69	7.83

ing ones that had been put up for adoption. The mean number of children for the whole group was 1.27. For blacks the mean number of children was 1.29, for whites 1.08, and for Hispanics 2.0. The American Indian woman had no children. Many of these women also had had several pregnancies that had resulted in miscarriages or abortions. Fifty percent of the women had five or more siblings. Fifty-nine percent of the blacks, 25 percent of the whites, and all the Hispanics had five or more siblings. The American Indian woman had eight siblings. Seventy-two percent of the women were single at the time of the interview: 83 percent of the blacks, 58 percent of the whites, and 50 percent of the Hispanics. The Native American woman had never been married. Only six women were married at the time of the interviews and none of these were living with their husbands.

When GEDs (Graduate Equivalency Diplomas usually obtained in juvenile detention or prison) are included in the calculations as twelve years of schooling completed, the mean number of years of schooling completed is 11.25. When the last year of regular schooling completed is used, the mean number of years of schooling drop to 10.69 years. According to this measure black women had completed 10.53 years of schooling, whites 11.08 years, and Hispanics 10.5 years. The American Indian woman had dropped out of school after completing the ninth grade.

Many of the women had had straight jobs at one time or another, but few had worked for very long. Including both part-time and full-time work and work engaged in under the Huber Law, the mean duration of longest employment for the entire sample was 7.83 months: 7.53 months for blacks, 9.71 months for whites, 2.17 months for Hispanics, and, for the American Indian woman, 2 months.

CHAPTER
II
Deviant Street Networks: The Social Context of Female Street Hustling

Most street hustling is carried out in the context of deviant street networks. By a deviant street network I mean a selection of individuals mobilized in relation to specific illicit ends. Such a network has fluid boundaries, may or may not have a real nucleus, and can be activated for relatively short or for extended periods of time.[1] Network activity revolves around all sorts of clever scams, but includes prostitution, petty larceny, forgery, credit card fraud, embezzlement, auto theft, drug traffic, burglary, and robbery. I would argue that only by becoming integrated into one or more deviant street networks can a street hustler make a

1. The definition of a deviant street network I use here differs from that contained in the work of Cohen by that title (1980) in the following way. There it refers to "the relationships between patterns of visible street deviance, the police, and the wider ecological and social environment" and explicitly does not include "the personal social psychological interactions among participants of a particular street condition" (3). I do not mean to suggest that police officers may not be part of deviant street networks, nor that I am unconcerned with the wider social and ecological environment. However, when I use the term, I intend to denote exactly that which Cohen excludes. Cohen's definition is completely appropriate for his analysis, which is predominantly ecological. Given the more general work in the area of social networks and the broader scope of the work at hand, however, the usage employed here seems more appropriate.

living by a hustle.[2] This is especially true for females, who are disadvantaged in terms of illegitimate opportunities in many of the same ways that they are disadvantaged with regard to legitimate opportunities.[3]

Network Structure and Functions

Deviant street networks are the context within which the hustling activity of women is structured and carried out. In Milwaukee networks differ with regard to focus, size, and composition. The portrait of network activity depicted here has been gathered from interviews with female street hustlers and, thus, it details in depth only those portions of networks that impinge on the careers of female street hustlers. It is impossible, however, to speak of the functions of deviant street networks in all their complexity as backdrops for, and motivating and controlling forces in, the careers of street women without reference to the network activity of men, for men clearly dominate such networks.

Generally speaking, the major function of deviant street networks is to facilitate street hustling as an income-producing strategy for those with whom one has historically engaged in such activity or those who have been identified as likely future partners in such endeavors. These networks often focus on a particular sort of street activity, such as dealing drugs, although they can be mobilized for other illegal pursuits as well. Through deviant street networks, information about opportunities to make money on a hustle and potential threats to one's ability to do so either by the authorities or non-network hustlers is disseminated. They are especially important in helping one learn to tell whether or not a

2. By using street jargon here I do not mean to imply that all female street hustlers make a living by doing what they do. Most of them have more than just themselves to support since they are also members of a domestic network or extended family household that includes children. Despite claims to the contrary, street life offers neither a secure nor a "good" living. Women on the street usually are also receiving welfare and may be working a straight job. Moreover, money must also be paid both to a "man" for protection, emotional support, and often drugs and, on occasion, to various agents of social control, including vice officers.

3. See Steffensmeier and Kokenda (1979), for example, for a discussion of the ideas of male thieves concerning the thieving capabilities of women and their trustworthiness as partners in crime.

potential victim is a vice cop by hugging him in such a way as to detect his "piece" (gun), when a bust is "coming down" (about to occur), when a chance to make "a piece of money" (perhaps twenty dollars or more) is about to present itself, or whom to go to for health care when your very need of it betrays your involvement in some illegal activity. In addition to being a source of information, deviant street networks may be a source of socio-emotional support, self-esteem, and courage. They are often also the locus of behavior that is exploitative, manipulative, and physically brutalizing.

In Milwaukee, there is an extensive set of deviant networks whose controlling members are predominantly black males in their mid to late twenties and early thirties. These men are likely to have lengthy criminal records such that future encounters with the law would almost certainly result in extended prison terms. As a result, they attempt to confine themselves to criminal activity that is not easily detected although they may deal in drugs or engage in other hustling activity. At least periodically, their major source of continuous income derives from the hustling activity of women who turn their earnings over to them in exchange for affection, an allowance, the status of their company, and some measure of protection, even if it is simply permission to use the man's name as a "keepaway" (from me) for other predatory men. These men form loose alliances to control the women who work for them, to promote their own hustling endeavors, and to socialize.

Each man has two or three women working for him. These individuals together form a pseudo-family. The women refer to each other as "wives-in-law" (the relationship of women one to the other who hustle for the same man) and to the male for whom they hustle as "my man" (a boyfriend for whom one hustles). To the degree that such men fear arrest and are successful in establishing such an arrangement, they are able to live "the fast life" (a life that is organized in pursuit of quickly obtained money) with limited risk. Although these men often fit the stereotype of the pimp in appearance, lifestyle, and income source, it is rare for them to procure "johns" (customers) for their women. Many of these women do work as prostitutes, but there is some diversity in their hustling activity. One woman I spoke with described a situation in which she worked primarily as a prostitute at the same time that one of her wives-in-law "busted paper" (forged) and the other "boosted" (shoplifted).

In his work on heterosexual prostitution in New York City, Bernard Cohen attempts to delimit a typology of "deviant managers." It is his belief that a key factor distinguishing a "man" from a pimp is that the former works together with one, rather than many, prostitutes. He may be the prostitute's lover or husband, and he shares the proceeds from prostitution. Unlike the professional pimp, the "man" provides immediate, on-the-spot protection and supervision. He watches his "woman" (a particular female who hustles for a particular man) constantly, is present where and when she works, and serves as a lookout for the police. In addition, he provides protection for his "woman" from robbery, assault, or other criminal victimization. Since a pimp cannot easily supervise or protect several women at once, he is more likely to establish overall guidelines. For example, he may insist that his women work near each other so that they can provide mutual assistance. Cohen argues that a pimp carries out managerial functions, while a "man" performs line supervision. A woman works *for* a pimp, but *with* a "man." Cohen notes that in New York the "man" tends to dress in ordinary, often shabby, street clothes rather than in flashy clothing in an attempt to blend in with the local street population. He is less likely than the pimp to be black and more likely to manage an older prostitute. Moreover, the "man" himself tends to be younger than the pimp. "Men" are more likely to manage prostitutes who work in relatively depressed socio-economic areas where a variety of hustling activity occurs, whereas pimps appear to manage prostitutes who work higher socio-economic areas at locations used nearly exclusively for purposes of prostitution (1980: 55–59).

Cohen's description provides a backdrop against which similar phenomena in Milwaukee can be examined. First, it is clear that the women in Milwaukee who would be classified as prostitutes using Cohen's methodology are often involved in a variety of other hustling activities as well.[4] Moreover, the life histories

---

4. It is possible that the diversity found in Milwaukee reflects the fact that the demand for prostitution there is not sufficient to support such specialization. Alternatively Cohen's methodology (1980), which was observation from an automobile, may have prevented him from viewing the hustling phenomenon in New York in all its diversity.

gathered in Milwaukee also indicate that the nature of these activities may change in response to the efforts of agents of social control, because new opportunities present themselves, or for personal reasons such as pregnancy. They may change over the career of the female hustler as well. Second, whereas Cohen posits two discrete types of deviant manager, the pimp and the "man," the descriptions of the behaviors, physical appearance, and preferred organizational form described to me by women who work for and with such men in Milwaukee lead me to posit a continuum of types of male managers rather than a dichotomy. At one end is the pimp, a flamboyant male who manages a "stable" (group of prostitutes) in a fairly bureaucratic way. At the other extreme is the "man," who is the husband/lover of the woman and really does work with her. In Milwaukee there are many more examples of intermediate types than of either the pure "pimp" or pure "man" types. In fact, the completely specialized "pimp" type does not seem to exist in Milwaukee at all. It may be that in a smaller city like Milwaukee, where the effort and success of social control agents in the area of vice is greater, this sort of bureaucratic structure has more difficulty emerging. Alternatively, it is possible that the women in a smaller city are less likely to work for a manager as a result of a deal that is almost entirely of a business sort or that they are reluctant to admit that this is the case. In any event, women interviewed rarely referred to a current manager as "my pimp." He was always referred to as "my man." For the female at least, the personal side of the relationship far outweighed the business side in importance. As a matter of fact, one of the most common reasons for a "woman" to leave a "man" was when some occurrence made it obvious that the relationship, from his point of view, was entirely for business purposes. On such occasions, women would say, "He wasn't nothin' but a pimp," or "Nobody knows how to spend my money better than me." The implication of these remarks was that the woman felt cheated and betrayed. Along these same lines, an oft-repeated statement was some variant of the following: "It don't take a smart man to be a pimp, only a dumb bitch."

On the other hand, the "man" does exist in Milwaukee and, as Cohen suggests, he and his women do tend to work in relatively depressed socio-economic areas. At least as far as street-level prostitution is concerned, two of the three major areas frequented by prostitutes are in the core center city neighborhoods described in Chapter I from which many of the women come. The other is a downtown area. The arrangement associated with "men" seems to be especially typical of prostitution-related hustling activity among Hispanics, for whom its occurrence probably has something to do with the limitations a lack of fluency in English places on a woman who tries to enter the competitive world of street hustling on her own and with similar limitations confronted by the less than fluent male who attempts to recruit and control several women. It may also reflect a greater possessiveness on the part of Hispanic men, even of a woman who prostitutes.[5] In addition, this type seems to be especially characteristic of addicted couples where the man may truly fear for his woman's safety or may be concerned that without close surveillance the woman who has completed a successful hustle will either be "ripped off" (robbed) or will "score" (obtain the drugs) and "shoot" (inject herself) without him.

The most common deviant manager types to be found in Milwaukee fall between these extremes. The descriptions provided by the women interviewed also indicate a dynamic rather than a static pattern of both deviant managers and deviant management. Males may begin their careers in deviant management over and over again as "men" only later to approach the "pimp" type with the addition of one or two wives-in-law to work with their "bottom woman." What appears to occur in Milwaukee is a trend toward the "pimp" form as the deviant manager attempts to enlarge his stable. This trend is continually subverted, however, by police activity and by the demands for more personal relationships by the women.[6]

5. It is important to note that, when the street hustling activity of Hispanic women takes this form, these women are insulated from the networks alluded to in the text and, as a result, have fewer hustling opportunities open to them.

6. Theoretically, the pure "pimp" form can only exist when the male has no reason to pretend that a personal relationship exists between him and each of the women who works for him or rarely risks having the true instrumental nature of the relationships revealed. The mere addition of new women undermines any semblance of individualized affection. This means that only males who can afford to maintain their own standard of living as successful pimps and reward their women handily as well are relieved of the burden of having to pretend to care for each woman. Financial success of this sort seems to be unachievable in a city like Milwaukee where the agents of social control are much more likely to be able to do their work effectively than they are in a larger city.

A common pattern over time is one in which one woman and her lover, who has recently been released from prison, start to generate an income based on her prostitution. At the same time, he begins hustling on his own, maybe selling a little "weed" (marijuana). He has become her "man" and, depending on her level of awareness and audience, she will acknowledge him as such. With increased income and greater freedom from the risk of arrest and the hard work of streetwalking a possibility, the woman may be persuaded to take a wife-in-law. As a result, the first woman becomes "bottom woman." This status entitles her to work less both on the street and at home because of the additional income and help with housework that comes with the other woman. It also may make her a manager in her own right, although one subordinate to the "man." At a later stage, a second wife-in-law may be recruited. Usually these new wives-in-law are relatively new at street hustling because they are easier to control than more streetwise women, such women can demand a higher price from johns than older hookers, and the group is less likely to suffer a loss of income due to a lengthy prison term if she is arrested. From the man's point of view, this is a desirable arrangement because having more women enhances his prestige, increases his income, and reduces his risk and his work. In addition, he has probably obtained a new sexual partner in the deal.

His main problem, then, is one of social control. He especially needs to meet the sexual and socio-emotional needs of his women without creating in-fighting and jealousy among them. Sometimes he may want to encourage a certain amount of discord among his women as a means of controlling them or at least to dissuade them from ganging up on him. If he is unsuccessful in achieving this delicate balance or is arrested, the pseudo-family dissolves. It may also break up due to the active intervention of one of the women. It is not uncommon for a jealous woman to put one of her wives-in-law in a situation that leads to her arrest. Also, to the extent that a man's women know about their man's hustling activities, they have some power over him. Vice officers will often offer not to arrest a female street hustler in exchange for information about her "man." Although a "woman" and her "man" may be together for quite some time, anywhere from a few months to several years, then, these pseudo-families are inherently unstable and are thus unlikely to survive for very long.

When they dissolve, the women may become part of other pseudo-families or begin a one-to-one relationship with another "man." Upon release from prison, a male may similarly attempt to hook up with one of his former "women" and be her "man" until he finds a suitable woman to be her wife-in-law. A female may also seek out her former "man" after release from jail or prison, pregnancy, illness, or an attempt to go straight or hustle alone. Then the cycle begins anew.

The desire for greater financial rewards and a more stable income, more prestige, less work, and fewer risks, then, prompts both men and women to form pseudo-families. Nonetheless, many of the women who come to the street are looking for caring relationships. What results is often a form of association that carries within itself the seeds of its own destruction. There are just too many ways in which the instrumental nature of the arrangement overrides the affectional aspirations of the women. Even the recruitment strategy employed by "men" sets them up for failure as pimps. Many of the women recruited are particularly vulnerable to males who project a caring, almost fatherly, demeanor because they are runaways or because they come from deeply troubled families. (This might explain Cohen's observation that pimps are more likely to manage younger women.) "Men" who recruit females using this fatherly ploy, however, are particularly vulnerable to being uncovered as exploiters at a later date. Older women are less likely to agree to be wives-in-law or to believe such lines than are younger women, who may not even know what a wife-in-law is.

Males who work the streets have a certain affinity for each other and benefit from the alliances they form. The more they approach the pure "pimp" form in terms of their relationships with their women and their own personal style, the more likely they are to form alliances among themselves on this basis. To do so enhances their ability to control the women who work for them and to control the efforts of new "men" to set up similar pseudo-families or even to begin working with a single "woman." If they are not actually involved in the street life themselves and confine their own hustling activity to low-risk pursuits, such as high-level drug dealing, this control can be accomplished fairly safely from afar. Managers currently working one on one with women on the street are much less likely to form networks with other men on this basis because they are much more clearly in direct competition with one another.

One kind of network is that formed by men as they approach the pure "pimp" end of the continuum described here. These networks are based on the management and exploitation of two or more women. The men involved in these networks may also be involved in networks from which women are usually excluded because to include them would be to give them a source of power "men" would rather they not have. These male networks may be transient or long-term depending on the particular hustling activity, the risk of arrest, and the potential rewards. Common activities might include burglary, forgery, fencing stolen goods, drug trafficking, and trafficking in guns, credit cards, or stolen cars or car parts. In addition, networks also evolve as a result of the contact that female street hustlers have with one another on the street and with the men they come in contact with while socializing with their "man" or while working. These women may be involved in deviant networks that include kin and fictive kin of both sexes and others as well. The networks formed by younger males and females alone, however, tend to focus more on the conditions of their own immediate deviant work and are more temporary and fluid than those formed by older male hustlers. It is often in the interest of these older male hustlers to attempt to undermine the networks formed by females and younger men and, indeed, women are often beaten when relationships that might develop into such networks are uncovered.

The Careers of Female Street Hustlers and Deviant Street Networks: Two Illustrative Cases

The general structure and functioning of deviant street networks themselves become clearer when we examine in some detail the careers of two female street hustlers. To understand these women's stories, it is necessary to shift our attention from the context of the deviant activities to the *ways in which those activities themselves are patterned over time* within the context of such networks. An additional dimension of this phenomenon will then come into focus—that is, the interface between deviant street networks and the actual personal considerations and contingencies (including deviant street network relationships) that shape the course of female street hustlers' careers. This discussion should also highlight the strength of network ties as they compete with or reinforce other personal and familial ties. The two cases presented below were chosen with an eye to illustrating the variation among the women interviewed in the sequence of activities engaged in during the years they hustled a living on the streets and the sorts of relationships they were involved in during that time.

Sandra

Although her career was at a temporary standstill at the time we spoke because she was in the last trimester of her first pregnancy, there is every reason to believe that at twenty-three Sandra is not yet ready to retire from street life. The deviant career line sketched here, then, is probably not complete. However, Sandra got an early start in "the life," and the extent of her criminal involvement to date has been such that the shape and direction of the course of that career are already discernible.

Sandra was born in a small town of approximately 1,500 people north of Madison. Although she was born in the United States, her parents were immigrants from Norway. She was the fourth of seven children. Her father, who now owns his own construction company, was a construction worker when she was growing up. Her mother worked in the home until Sandra was about six years old. Then she took a job as a practical nurse in a county institution for the elderly.

Although her parents were not church-goers, Sandra was forced to attend Lutheran Sunday School and claims that her parents were generally quite strict with her. She started having disagreements with her father that escalated into physical battles when she was about nine years old. Her father apparently went from being a moderate drinker to being a very heavy drinker at about this time. When he had been drinking, he would accuse Sandra of sleeping with neighborhood boys and call her a "whore." She claims that there was no basis for such accusations. She apparently looked to her mother for protection from her father's wrath, but found no ally in her. Rather, Sandra describes her mother as generally ineffectual and passive when confronted with her husband's fury.

After one particularly heated fight, Sandra asked her guidance counselor at school to put her in touch with the county department of social services because she did not want to live at home any longer. She wanted to be placed in foster care. She ended up spending the night in the county jail because she refused to return home and, in any event, her father refused to let her come home. She was placed in foster care the next day and stayed with her foster family for six months. She then ran away because she says she was disgusted with the inferior treatment she received from her foster parents when compared with the treatment given their daughter by birth.

When she was apprehended by the sheriff's department, she was placed with another family. This time, she claims not to have liked the school she was placed in. Shortly after enrolling, she was expelled for being truant, uncooperative, and disrespectful. This time she was sent to a school for emotionally disturbed children. Shortly after her arrival, the school lost its license and closed.

At this point, Sandra was transferred to a state mental facility in Mendota. When she was at Mendota, she became friendly with several young women from Madison. At one point she ran away from that institution with them. The group headed for Madison, and it was during her short stay there that she became acquainted with a variety of counterculture people and institutions that offered various sorts of formal and informal services for runaways. After she had been at Mendota for about five months, an attempt was made to reunite Sandra and her family. She stayed at home for about two weeks, had another fight with her father, during which he beat her, and was on the run again.

When apprehended, again in Madison, she was sent to a state institution for delinquent girls in Oregon, Wisconsin, by the juvenile court. She had been adjudicated "uncontrollable" and "habitually truant." Sandra had just turned twelve when she arrived at Oregon for a six-month stay. There she met some young women who like herself had committed status offenses and some who had been convicted of criminal offenses. These women had been involved in prostitution, shoplifting, forgery, and other mercenary offenses. She says of this time: "My education was all in Oregon. I met people that did it all, you know; I heard talkin' and I knew, if I had to, I could do it too."

When Sandra was released from Oregon, she went home again. This time, she stayed a month. She had become close to several young black women in Oregon and had started to hang with blacks and to see a young black man. This was utterly intolerable behavior from her father's point of view. She ran away to Madison again, was apprehended, and returned to Oregon, this time for a year.

Sandra claims that the first time she was in Oregon, she "pretty much went along with the program and stayed in the background." This time, however, she became actively involved in all the "craziness" that occurred there. She describes being put in lock-up, participating in a riot, and helping to set a fire in the institution. She ran away several times, and each time she returned, she would be given additional time. She would run to Madison or to Milwaukee and look up women she had met in the institution.

When she was thirteen, she ran away and stayed away for six months. She came to Milwaukee and started "turning tricks" (completing acts of prostitution) to survive. She also started drinking and smoking marijuana fairly regularly at about this time. While in Milwaukee, she lived with a young woman whom she had met in Oregon and the woman's boyfriend. The man would bring customers home to have sex with his girlfriend and Sandra. Because she didn't "walk the stroll" (walk up and down streets known to be frequented by prostitutes in the hope of picking up a customer who is on foot or in a car), she never caught a case for prostitution or anything else during this particular absence from Oregon.

When she was sixteen and once again on the run from Oregon, she met a young black man who was the boyfriend of another woman she knew from the institution. She describes the situation this way:

> He ran across some paper and some ID, and I started bustin' checks. We did it all over the states of Wisconsin, Michigan, Illinois, and Minnesota. We had about ten thousand dollars when we were finished. None of it was saved; it was, ah, it was on cars and apartments and getting high, and stuff. I got caught. I had one check left out of the whole bunch that we had, and we already had all of this money. And I got greedy with it. I knew that it was probably hot and I would get busted, but I took a chance. I needed five hundred more

dollars and I could get a lot of shit with it. I didn't . . . I was
still at the point in my life where I was used to spending
money . . . which I still am now . . . and spending it the
way I want to . . . and having stuff I want to have. I've never
worked a job except when I've been in jail on Huber Law
[work release].

They sent Sandra back to Oregon, where she was kept in lock-up.
She says: "They were trying to waiver [sic] my rights as a juvenile,
chargin' me as an adult for these checks 'cause it was a tri-state
thing and other people were involved and a lot of cash from the
checks. I was the only one that got busted."

While she was still in lock-up awaiting a hearing, Sandra's
four-year-old nephew died and she was given permission to
return home. Instead of taking the bus home, Sandra caught a bus
for Milwaukee because she felt certain that, once she returned to
Oregon, she would be tried as an adult, convicted, and sent to
Taycheedah. She went to Milwaukee and worked as a prostitute
out of the house of the friends she had worked with previously. As
soon as she had enough money to buy a few items of clothing and
a plane ticket to Miami and still have a few hundred dollars'
savings, she headed south. She describes her activities after arriving as follows:

> I had a girlfriend of mine that lived there. She was workin'
> the streets, and her boyfriend and her were doin' real good.
> And, so, I met her and worked. That's the first time I ever
> worked the streets, you know, which was a bit of a stroll:
> Miami Beach, 163rd and Collins Avenue, a big stroll, huge.
> My feet hurt along with everything else. The first couple of
> months I was down there I was dealing all by myself, you
> know. I didn't have to be, but I was making money setting
> up my own deals. And then, after a while, I started going
> with a guy, and he was nothin' but a pimp, you know, a
> player, or whatever. It was the first time I ever really paid,
> but at this time I felt that I needed to 'cause I needed him for
> protection more than anything else, you know, on the strip
> down there . . . from the other pimps. 'Cause they were killin'
> girls down there, you know, at a steady rate. It happened
> a lot, and it almost happened to me one time. A guy took me

way out and took all my clothes and beat me. They did find
a girlfriend of mine dead on the beach. I got to be really
scared. And so, I started going with this guy named Al who
had a couple of other ladies at the time.

Sandra stayed with Al for almost a year. During that time,
he went from being an occasional drug user to shooting heroin
regularly. When he was high, he began to beat the women who
worked for him, including Sandra. He finally beat one of his
women to death and received a life sentence.

Sandra was puzzled by this change in his behavior. She says:
"When I met him, he was a person that would never lay a hand on
me. He was just . . . I don't know . . . he was pretty enough and
nice enough, you know, to make a woman obedient to him without beating them. I was with him for about a year when the
beatings started, and I left and I was living on the beach then.
Then I moved to Hollywood" (Florida). During her time with Al,
Sandra started to use hard drugs herself. Although she didn't
shoot, she did begin to snort cocaine regularly. After leaving Al,
Sandra caught a case for prostitution while attempting to work
out of a major Miami hotel. She used an assumed name when she
was arrested, however, and had enough money to get herself out
of jail on bond and, eventually, to pay her fine. She found that, by
paying the maitre d' at that hotel twenty dollars every evening,
she could safely work the hotel. As a result of this arrangement,
she began to make about five hundred dollars a night.

About four months later, she ran into Al at a party and
"instantly" went back with him. She claims to have had ten thousand dollars saved at that point, which she turned over to him.
Sandra says she went back with Al primarily because she was
lonely. She says:

So I was with him once again and on the street once again.
Things started to get hot and we started to travel . . . traveling, traveling to Atlanta, to different part of Florida, all
over. We went to all these different places; we went across
the country, you know. I did that for I'd say a little over
three months. And the beatings got bad again and the shit
just got bad. It got to the point where he wasn't even paying
me the attention that I really needed, you know. It was the

only thing I really demanded, the attention, and he wasn't giving me that.

During this time Sandra also turned eighteen so that future run-ins with the law would have much more serious consequences In any event, she decided that she wanted to return to Wisconsin. She called the administrator at Oregon, the district attorney in Milwaukee, and the woman who had been her social worker when she first started to fight with her father. From the information she received from these people, she concluded that she could come back to Wisconsin without risk of arrest. Sandra describes her homecoming this way:

> So I hopped on a Greyhound bus, and I came back to Wisconsin. I came to Madison. There were still people there that I knew from before. There was one bar that I had always gone to, that I had been going to ever since I was young. So I just came back to town, got a motel room, went down there and met all of my friends. And I had a few thousand dollars . . . ah, I had enough to survive on. I didn't have to bust my ass.

Very quickly Sandra's money ran out, however, and she started working at a topless bar. She was also collecting General Assistance (welfare). She says:

> Not that there wasn't anything in Madison on the street, but this was safer . . . 'cause most of the customers came from the bar . . . which wasn't really makin' a livin', but it was . . . I was surviving, being on welfare, too. I really didn't have that much to worry about; it was only me. And I started going with a guy that I met in Madison. He was working, making three or four hundred dollars every two weeks. And, it got to be all right, but I wasn't . . . I couldn't spend his money the way I wanted to spend money. I wanted to have my own.

Because of her desire to have her own money, Sandra recruited a female partner and, together, they started an escort service. They took ads in the local newspaper, hired four women, got

themselves a phone, and they were in business. Sandra describes
her first entrepreneurial venture as follows:

> It turned out to be really the most profitable thing I've ever
> done and the least risky 'cause it was, ah, nothin' under sixty
> dollars. You just got in there and you got paid sixty dollars.
> It was always a hundred dollars, a hundred fifty dollars, two
> hundred dollars, and just working over the phone; it was
> easy. We employed, over a two-and-a-half-year period,
> about twenty different girls. At any one time, we had four.
> We always had two white girls, with different color hair, a
> blond and a brunette, and we tried to keep two black girls.
> And then myself, which was just once in a while. I eventu-
> ally ended up hiring a girl just to sit and answer the phone.
> And we got a beeper system. So everybody had a beeper; they
> just didn't have to sit around; they could go out and do what
> they wanted to do and just get a call. The calls were sixty
> dollars minimum. I took twenty dollars off every call, and
> we gave the girl whatever she got, and we paid the recep-
> tionist five dollars for every call. And it was a lot of money;
> it was good money. If I went out, it was like . . . sometimes
> it was a thousand dollars a night.

Sandra and her boyfriend Jack accumulated quite a bit of
money as a result of the escort service, his straight job, and his
hustling. He was a gambler. They bought a brand-new blue Eldorado, jewelry, and clothes. Then Jack was arrested during a craps
game. He was on parole at the time. That meant that a new
conviction could put him back in prison for quite a long time. At
the same time, Sandra and two of the women who worked for her
were also arrested. The attorneys' fees wiped them out financially.
Shortly afterwards, Jack was arrested again, this time for first-
degree murder. He was accused of slitting the throat of the man
who ran the craps house. They had a history of not getting along,
and Jack's blue Eldorado had been seen near the spot where the
body was found.

      While he was in jail, Sandra went to Muskegon, Michigan,
to work in a house of prostitution in order to raise funds for her
boyfriend's defense. She made three thousand dollars there in a
little over three weeks and went back to Madison and gave the

money to Jack's lawyer. Then she left again and headed for Florida. This time Sandra went to Tampa, however, rather than Miami because she didn't want to run into Al, the man who used to pimp her. She took a woman inexperienced in street life with her whom she pimped. After making about four thousand dollars there, she came back to Madison. In Madison, she conned a trick out of another thousand. All this money Sandra then turned over to Jack's attorney. Meanwhile the escort service was still in operation. Sandra says:

> I was still trying to run the service. We needed it even more than we did before, and things were getting hot. I got busted for prostitution. Eventually his court date came up, and he was acquitted. Then he had to lie pretty low, and the money was getting a little tighter. I was still with him. Eventually, the police closed up the service, and I started working in all the hotels. Then, in seventy-seven, we got busted for selling drugs. I sold twenty amphetamines to an undercover agent, and he set up the sale. We both got arrested for it. I pleaded guilty; he pleaded innocent. He got convicted of conspiracy and went to prison. He's still there; he got three years because he still had some time left on parole. So they took him to Waupun [state penal facility for men]. I got nine months in jail and three years' probation. And I went to county jail and did my nine months. I had Huber Law [work release], though, so after three or four months, I went and applied for a job at a small dress shop, and got it. It was just bookkeeping for an office, but . . . you got to go out every day, and smoke some grass, and see people. I got out in July of seventy-eight.

After her release from jail, Sandra became involved with a man she had known for quite some time, "but had never dealt with romantically." He was a heavy drug user and dealer. Sandra started to become a very serious drug user herself, shooting cocaine, heroin, and speed. She says she wasn't happy even though her boyfriend was providing for all her needs, including her need for drugs. About this time, she went to Milwaukee to attend a concert. She was busted for marijuana and carrying a concealed weapon (a knife). While in jail, she became very ill. She was taken to the hospital, where she was informed that she was pregnant. Sandra describes this time as follows:

> I had to stay in the hospital about a week. When I got out, my PO [probation officer] told me he was going to send me to TY [Taycheedah], but since I was pregnant, he would give me a good break and send me here [the halfway house where the interview was recorded].

Sandra was upset that the father of the baby she was carrying was the man she had most recently been involved with and not her boyfriend in prison at Waupun. She says: "Well, when he gets out, you know, he'll come to where I am. I mean . . . we plan on getting married. We'll try to get married while I'm here and he's in Waupun, within the next couple of months, before the baby's born."

Sandra herself claims to have plans to enter the University of Wisconsin–Madison in the fall (the interview was completed in the summer) and to transfer to the LaCrosse campus in January, by which time her baby would have been born and she would be off probation. She wants to move to LaCrosse because she "knows some people there." The idea is to finish out her first year of school there and "try to transfer, you know, maybe to the University of Florida."

Although one might assume that Sandra's plan to further her education and marry indicates a desire to leave the fast life behind, this is clearly not the case. She neither wants to nor, even if she did, is she likely to. The people she knows in LaCrosse are hustlers and Sandra will surely begin to hustle again once she reestablishes her association with them. She will probably become involved with another "man." If she does have another romantic involvement, it will most likely be with a male "in the life" for she feels that she would have little in common with a "square." Nor does she feel that she can return home or expect any support from her family. She has not been in contact with any of the members of her family for six years. As far as she knows, none of them have had any serious run-ins with the law during that time. For that reason, and because of her relationship with them in the past, she has no reason to believe that they would be any more sympathetic to her now than they were six years ago. Unless they were to get in touch with her, and that seems highly unlikely, her feelings about their reactions preclude her reaching out to them for support.

Sandra's decision, then, would not be made in isolation. The men in her life would clearly be a force that would most likely propel her back into some form of hustling as would a lack of support for alternate behavior. Most importantly, however, Sandra does not see the choice to go to college as one that rules out hustling. It is simply something to do until she is off probation that will allow her legitimately to absent herself from the halfway house. It is also an idea that sits well with the counselors in the house and makes her life there a little easier. Beyond this, she has only a vague idea that her education would be something to fall back on should she be unable to hustle. She claims to want to become a social worker and counsel delinquent girls. She doesn't seem to realize that future involvement with the law may make this difficult even if she does complete her schooling. She obviously has gained a certain amount of self-confidence and independence during her life on the streets despite the fact that she admits that it was often very hard. She is not very confident about her ability to make a living at a straight job, however, nor is she very sure she wants to. Sandra has come to take a certain pride in her ability to earn a living on a hustle and seems almost disdainful of those who tie themselves to the routine demanded by "regular work." She says:

> I lived with a girl who was working a regular job, and she said, "Fuck it." I was home all the time, and she was working all the time, but I had oodles more money than she did. I introduced her to some people and she starting working [hustling]. And it took her a while to get . . . her insides, you know, ready for it and accustomed to it, you know. But she's never lived the way she lives now. And she's happy with herself. She's not down on herself. If you're down on yourself, then it's just making you miserable.

Sandra has been able to acquire at least some of the material things that she has wanted and needed as a result of her hustling. She really doesn't seem to be able to envision herself making a living any other way. Immediately after relating her plans to attend college in the fall, for example, Sandra said:

I can't say I'll stop workin' [hustling]; I don't think I'll ever stop it. If the opportunity comes up and someone offers me enough money, I'll do it. You know, I'm used to livin' a certain kinda way. I mean, I don't think I'll ever walk the stroll again, but I'll do anything else. If I have to feed my baby, I will, you know? I know I can. I know I can survive anywhere. I've never wanted for money . . . I don't think I ever want to go to PTA meetings, you know. But I still want to be married and live in my own house. I wouldn't want a little cottage; I want a mansion. My tastes and my expectations are still right up there. And I will make compromises, you know; I don't have to have every luxury in the world. But, you know, like cable TV and a dishwasher and basic shit . . . my clothes cleaned when they're dirty . . . and be able to eat and be able to go out and buy a few drinks when I want and not have to worry about it . . . and have a car, a half-way decent car, a nice car, you know, not beat-up and ready to fall apart. I think if I could afford a maid to do the cleaning, she would do the cleaning and the laundry and the dishes. But, I would cook, maybe . . . not all the time. But, I'll cook; I like to cook. If I was living in a big enough house . . . I'll settle for a small house and me and Jack and the kid and everything. As long as I'm comfortable, I mean . . . a home . . . as long as I have what I want to have.

Betsy

Betsy is the same age as Sandra, twenty-three. Even though she started hustling about four years later, at age eighteen, she clearly has many more physical and emotional scars as a result of her life on the street than Sandra does. Physically, the only thing they share are the heroin tracks on their forearms. Sandra is a tall, attractive strawberry blond who is bright and at least projects a certain self-confidence. During our interview, she puffs comfortably on a cigarette. Betsy is a wiry little black woman with a face severely scarred on one side from injuries she sustained when a trick pushed her onto the highway from a speeding car. She has almost no hair, having badly burned her scalp several months earlier when she applied a delousing salve to it and left it on much longer than prescribed. She had shot some Ts and Blues (a combination of Talwin and Pyribenzamine) and ingested some pills she bought on the street and had hallucinated that her hair was crawling with bugs. Unlike Sandra, Betsy is wary and sometimes confused. During the interview she peeks out at me from under the red bandanna that covers her shorn head. Her life has had all the lows that Sandra's has, plus some; it has had few of the highs. Although Sandra's street career is probably far from over, Betsy's will probably end in the not too distant future, not by choice, but because she has overdosed on drugs, received a lengthy sentence for a violent crime, or become a fatality in such a crime herself.

When we met, Betsy had recently been released from the House of Correction, where she had been held for six weeks because of her failure to pay outstanding fines for loitering, shoplifting, prostitution, and disorderly conduct. She has had multiple arrests for all these things and for possession of drugs, carrying a concealed weapon, and robbery. She claims not to have committed the robbery.[7] In any event, the robbery charges were dismissed. Betsy readily admits having been involved in forging checks, selling narcotics, and fencing stolen goods, although she has never been arrested for any of those acts.

During her stay at the House of Correction, Betsy had had a hearing on a more recent unpaid fine. At that time, the judge had reduced her overall indebtedness to the state by two-thirds. Consequently, when her next welfare check came, Betsy got herself out. There was a condition placed on this demonstration of judicial leniency, however, and that was that upon release Betsy enroll in a drug treatment program for ninety days. For the first two weeks of that period, Betsy was supposed to live at the treatment center while she became accustomed to the counseling regimen, was evaluated by the staff there, and located an apartment and a job. She was on probation and in the process of trying to accomplish all this when I interviewed her and she told me about her life.

Betsy has three older brothers. Compared to Sandra, who says that none of her siblings have had run-ins with the law, Betsy says of her siblings: "I have two brothers in Milwaukee and one in Connecticut. Now he's the type of fellow . . . marriage . . . the

7. It should be noted that it was very rare for female street hustlers to deny having committed a crime for which they had been arrested. As a result, in the cases where this occurred, my tendency was not to doubt them.

marriage type. He works so he don't be in law trouble. But the rest of us that's here, we in and outta jail."

Most of the time growing up Betsy lived with her brothers, her mother, her father, and a young female cousin. She remembers her mother and father having frequent fights although she doesn't recall what they were about. As long as she can remember, her mother alternated two-week drinking binges with longer periods of sobriety, remorse, and religious fervor. The fights between her parents became more violent as she approached her teens. She describes these events this way:

> My brothers use to be out. It seem every time they go out the house, they [Betsy's parents] use to fight because my brothers use to stop my father from jumpin' on my mother. All I could do was cry and scream: "Don't, please don't." I would just cry and run out the house and look for my brothers. And that hurt me a lot.

Betsy feels that her mother favored her brothers, whereas she was "daddy's girl." Some of the fights her parents had at this time seem to have been about how the children were turning out. The son who eventually moved to Connecticut had joined the Navy. The remaining two sons were beginning to get in trouble with the law. Betsy's father apparently blamed his wife for their delinquency. He also predicted that Betsy would "have ninety-nine kids" before she got out of school and stated repeatedly that, if that happened, it would be Betsy's mother's fault.

When Betsy was fourteen, her mother took her daughter and left her husband. He had become increasingly violent, and Betsy's mother's physician had recommended that, for her own safety, she leave him. They went to live with Betsy's brother in Hartford, Connecticut, for several months, but he made it clear that he was neither willing nor able to support them, and they returned to Milwaukee. Betsy's mother set up house with Betsy and her two brothers. Her cousin had moved out on her own. At this time, determined that her husband's prediction would not come true when she was in sole charge, Betsy's mother started to keep extra-close tabs on her. Betsy describes her mother's attempts to control her behavior as follows:

I didn't have a teenager's life. That's why when I turned eighteen, off I went. She let me out with a boyfriend when I was fifteen, and then when we broke up, she said I couldn't have no more men friends until I was eighteen. Okay, I use to skip school a lot, but she use to say how my father would say I'm gonna have ninety-nine kids before I get outta school. Okay, to prove to my father that my mother was worthy of taking care of us without me gettin' pregnant and this and that, I couldn't see men. I was still skippin' school, but I wasn't skippin' to have sex with nobody. It was just to have fun 'cause I knew when I got home, I couldn't have no fun like the rest of the young kids. They could go to social centers and stuff like that, and I couldn't go there. She wouldn't let me go out after school, and in the summer, you know, eight o'clock. If it was five minutes or even two minutes after eight, I would get "hookers" [slapped]. My other girlfriends got 'til ten o'clock, and we be right outside in front the house. It was hot and all that stuff. But she thought I was. . . . My first "date" [trick] was my first time having sex, and I was eighteen. My mother use to slip birth control pills to me because I was skippin' school and she thought I was doin' stuff like that. Yeah, and tellin' me they's vitamins.

When Betsy was fifteen, her mother took in her son Joey's newborn baby boy. At the time of the interview the child was eight years old and still in her care. The infant's mother, Marlene, was only a few years older than Betsy and had already been on the street for over a year. When the realities of Marlene's street life impinged on her own in such a dramatic way, Betsy's mother's response was to try to place even tighter controls on Betsy. She insisted that she be allowed to choose Betsy's clothes. Betsy describes them as "plain." They were not only not fashionable; "they were the ugliest clothes" Betsy says she had ever seen. Betsy's mother had always made her attend church services, but now she insisted that Betsy go to church not just once on Sundays, but twice. Betsy ran away. She was sixteen at the time. The police found her at the home of a cousin after having only been gone overnight.

Betsy's mother attempted to reason with her daughter. She tried to convince her that she should at least not ruin her chances of getting a high school diploma. Betsy completed her fourth year of high school and continued to live with her mother during this last year. She did not receive her diploma, however. Her English teacher refused to pass her because of her high rate of absenteeism in his class. Betsy went to summer school, but never completed the required course.

In the fall, Betsy got a job at a food-processing company. This was her first full-time job (she had worked at McDonald's part-time in high school, but had been fired for smoking marijuana on the job). She was working third shift and, once again, felt that she was "missin' out on things." About a month after she took this job, Marlene, the young woman whose child Betsy's mother was raising, suggested that Betsy get involved in prostitution. This happened one afternoon when the young woman was visiting her son at Betsy's house. Betsy had told her that she wanted more fun in her life as well as more money. Marlene reportedly said: "Well, just mess with the sailors; you don't have to do no other stuff." Marlene had recently left Betsy's brother, who had been her first "man" and who had beaten her. She was looking for another woman to work with for protection. She started taking Betsy with her to work the streets and the downtown Ramada Inn and Howard Johnson's Motor Lodge. Sailors from the Great Lakes Naval Base in northern Illinois were known to stay at these motels when they came to Milwaukee for the weekend or just the evening.[8] Within a few days, the two began to work regularly with two other young women they had met on the streets.

These four women worked together for several weeks. It was not long before all four of them had "men," however. Betsy was introduced to her "man" by Marlene's new "man." Betsy had been living with her "man" and her two wives-in-law for several

---

8. The sailors are correctly perceived by the female street hustlers as a particularly vulnerable and safe group to prey upon. They are very young and inexperienced, often have a good deal of cash on them, and are usually too embarrassed and scared of repercussions from the base to report robberies and the like to the police. Moreover, they are not thought to be as potentially dangerous to street women physically as more anonymous "tricks." As one woman said: "It's quick, clean, safe, and profitable."

months when the police and judges in Milwaukee initiated an intense effort to get tough with street hustlers. Betsy says of this time:

> They had just started this loitering stuff and they were so down on it, like every night they was pickin' up a truckload of girls. So the money had added up because every time you go, they raise it a hundred dollars, all the way to five hundred. Once you get to five hundred, every time you go, you get fined five hundred. I was wanted for a lot of money on the "runner" [concurrent] fines.

Because Milwaukee had become so inhospitable to street hustlers, Betsy, her "man," and her two wives-in-law went to work in Memphis and Nashville for a while. Betsy's "man" was originally from Tennessee, and it was his decision that they should go there. When things started to get hot for them there, they went to Florida, where they had heard there was quite a bit of money to be made hustling and in the drug trade.

Just before leaving Milwaukee, Betsy had been charged with the robbery of a trick referred to above. Her mother posted her bail. Betsy had been in court once before on this charge, but the man who was pressing charges failed to appear. The judge told her that if the complainant failed to appear for the next court date, the charges would be dismissed. Betsy decided to return for her court date. She wanted to clear her name because she claims not to have committed this crime. She also wanted to be able to return to Milwaukee without having a serious outstanding charge on her record. Moreover, she didn't want her mother to forfeit her bail money, although that was a minor concern because she says she could have reimbursed her mother.

She returned to Milwaukee right after having been pushed from the speeding car. The robbery charges were dismissed, and Betsy purchased her airline ticket to return to Florida. She was taking a nap at her mother's prior to going to the airport when she was arrested by several police officers for her outstanding fines. Her mother had called the police and turned her daughter in. She thought that Betsy's injuries had been inflicted by her "man." She said she didn't believe the story of her being pushed from the car. This was the only way she knew to prevent Betsy from returning to Florida.

Betsy spent about six weeks in the county jail. During this time, her "man" went to visit his family in Memphis and gave Betsy's wives-in-law a "vacation." They came to Milwaukee to see their families. Betsy called all of them to ask for money to pay her fines, but none of them would help her. Her brothers also refused to give her money. Her mother sent her three dollars a week pocket money.

When she got out of jail, Betsy decided to stay in Milwaukee. She started to walk the street alone. Her second night out she hooked up with a "man" who, after they had been together several weeks, began to beat her with coat hangers when he sensed she was withholding money from him. She says: "I had to hurry up and leave him alone because the hangers was really too much, and I felt he was really no boyfriend."

Then Betsy met a hustler in a tavern who needed a female partner to cash some stolen checks. She worked with him for a while and, after three months, discovered she was pregnant with his child. He was originally from Detroit. When he found she was going to have his child, he took her there to meet his family. Shortly after they arrived, a former "woman" of his tipped off the police that he was in town, and he was arrested for forgery, convicted, and imprisoned.

Betsy came home to have her baby. Her "man" was released when their baby was four months old. He came to Milwaukee to see Betsy and his daughter. While there, he heard from some other male hustlers that Betsy had been working as a prostitute during her pregnancy. Betsy denies this, saying she wouldn't have stooped so low as to work while pregnant. Still, he told her that since she had "done him dirty" when he was in prison, he now wanted nothing to do with her. (At the time of the interview, he had come to see his daughter one time since.) Betsy's mother began to take care of her new granddaughter, and Betsy was back on the street again.

Betsy had been introduced to hard drugs by one of the four women she first worked with. She had been a moderate user ever since. At this time she became such a heavy user of pills, heroin, cocaine, and the heroin substitute, Ts and Blues, that neither male nor female street hustlers wanted to work with her. She did have a relationship with one "man" during this time who was interested in having her work for him if she could get her drug use under control. Betsy had an excellent reputation on the street for busting paper, and this "man," Ron, apparently thought it was worth his effort to see if he couldn't help her curb her drug use. She describes the relationship as follows:

> He was a hustler. He had other ladies and I didn't have to do nothin'. I think I gave him two hundred dollars and we were together like six months. And like he had one lady that was a booster [shoplifter], and the other lady, he had her go to the bank [forge]. So I didn't have to do nothin' for him. He tried to get me off drugs, but I was still in my momma's house, okay? My momma and Joey didn't like him, never did like anybody I liked. My brothers really didn't like him because that just stopped them from gettin' a free high from me. Dumb me, listenin' to my family, tryin' to keep my family cool instead of listenin' to him tellin' me: "Don't go out stealin' and things because you don't know what you're doin' when you're high." 'Cause I was catchin' petty cases. He would come and get me, and, like I said, I didn't pay the man.

Ron was eventually arrested for forgery. As Betsy tells it: "They had all kinda counts on him; his bail was sky high." He was in jail over Christmas, and Betsy wanted to visit him, but a major snowstorm prevented her from doing so. Then she received a telegram from him saying that she shouldn't go to visit him at all because visitors are asked to show identification and are routinely checked for outstanding warrants, fines, and so forth.

Betsy continued to try to hustle on her own. Her drug use was completely out of control. She was very depressed because she didn't seem able to help the man who had helped her either financially or emotionally. The money she made went to support her drug habit, herself, and her family. Her brothers also expected her to "turn them on" (supply them with drugs) when she had drugs or they would slap her and otherwise physically threaten her. Her mother threatened to turn her over to the police or seek formal custody of her little girl if she didn't curtail her drug use and contribute more to the running of the household.[9] Betsy describes her state at this time:

> I went way down on account of drugs and stuff. I couldn't go no lower than what I was before I went into the House of Correction. I would get in a cab every day because I didn't have a friend, man or woman, to take me hustling. I'd tell the driver all my troubles. I didn't have nobody else. The cab, he would cost twenty or thirty dollars. I had the cab to worry to pay, then I would spend thirty or forty dollars for pills. Whatever type of money I made I just spent it on me and my family. I could make like two or three hundred dollars a day, and it would be gone. I might wake up with twenty dollars, and it was very hard to get money without gettin' picked up for loiterin' and shopliftin'. I'd be high and make mistakes and get knocked off.

Before Betsy was imprisoned in the House of Correction, Ron got out on bail:

> A friend of his finally went and got him out and without my help. They done told him a lot a bull stuff about me while he was in jail. I haven't seen him since, but he came by the house. I told my people I wasn't there. And so I got in the House [of Correction] and I got in contact with him because I saw he was a good man to me. He didn't let me do nothin'. But, yet, he got two girls who was doin' somethin' for him. But he just didn't want me to do nothin'. And so I felt that's the man I need to be with. And I was on the street goin' through all these changes. I didn't want him to see me like that. That's why I didn't contact him on the street. So now I want to talk to him. But, you know, he could just turn against me by saying I didn't try to help him when he was in need as good as he was to me and stuff.

9. She made similar threats to Betsy's nephew's mother. Formal custody would allow Betsy's mother to collect AFDC (Aid to Families with Dependent Children) benefits directly. It would, in turn, deprive Betsy and her brother's former "woman" of rights to AFDC benefits. They often used this money to pay fines and purchase drugs.

Betsy says that she really wants to "leave the drugs alone."
Ron might be able to help her do that. On the other hand, as she
says, "He's a hustler." Continued contact with him will almost
inevitably put her in touch with the world of drug users, as will
contact with her own family. Yet she sees nothing incompatible
about her desire to get a job, have her own apartment, and take
care of her little girl and her continued involvement with this
latest "man." She says:

> I'm going to see. But things don't be. . . . I know it's not
> going to be like it was. This time I know he'll have me
> bustin' paper or whatever. But if he do me wrong and stuff,
> then I'm gonna have to leave him alone because I know it'll
> be nothin' but a payback to him. But I'm gonna see when I
> get out the program. I told him about I was gonna get a job
> and stuff, too. But I could do a little paper for him on the
> side when I'm through workin' and stuff. When I'm in the
> drug clinic, I'm not gonna mess around with nothin', not
> 'til I get out this time.

Since Betsy is not opposed to "doin' a little paper" after
work and intends to try to reestablish a relationship with this
male hustler, it is almost certain that she is going to be back in the
fast life.

For Sandra, straight living lacks excitement; for Betsy no life
other than hustling is really conceivable. Despite their shared
problems of drug abuse, Sandra seems more self-assured and in
control than Betsy. In the past, drugs have ruled Betsy's life. They
have pushed her to increase her hustling activities at the same
time that they have diminished the chance that those activities
will have a very high rate of return. Although drug use may have
motivated Sandra to hustle, they have neither made it imperative
that she do so nor effectively made it impossible.

There is a certain desperate quality about Betsy, then, that
leaves her open to manipulation and victimization in a way Sandra is not. Whereas Sandra may take risks because they are exciting, Betsy seems to have little choice. As a result, despite the fact
that her recent time in the House of Correction has probably
substantially curtailed her drug use and despite her expressed
desire to stop using drugs, Betsy will probably continue to be a

user. This, along with her continued contact with deviant street networks through other hustlers including her brothers and her nephew's mother, the demands of her mother for money, and her own depressed value as a prostitute due to her physical state all predict involvement in more serious offenses as well as even greater drug use. Moreover, Betsy's risk of arrest and physical harm will both increase. Betsy will probably return rather quickly to street life, then, but that life may be a short one.

Variation in the Relationship between Hustling Activity and Its Social Context

The cases of Sandra and Betsy presented above illustrate the extremely diverse life circumstances that can result from the interaction between the personal and familial histories peculiar to each woman before and during involvement in street life and her hustling activity as it is shaped by the deviant street networks within which she hustles. The variation is not only apparent as one looks at the two cases, but over the course of each woman's life as well.

The cases of other women interviewed illustrate intermediate points on a continuum measuring how well or poorly they fared as hustlers at any particular point in time and over the course of their hustling careers. There are also many variables only hinted at in these two case histories such as physical attractiveness, general health, fertility, relationships with families/ households of origin, and run-ins with the criminal justice system that influence the course of their lives. The more important of these will be discussed in some detail in Chapter V, "Living the Fast Life." Their values and goals influence and are influenced by the deviant networks within which they work and their personal circumstances and histories. These factors are the topic of Chapter VI, "Dreams: Aspirations, Role Models, and Attitudes."

The major insight to be gained from the descriptions of the cases of Sandra and Betsy and the general theoretical discussion that preceded them, however, is that deviant street networks are continually imperiled and yet essential for the hustling activity of the women described in this book. They are both the means of their survival as street hustlers and a major source of their victimization.

CHAPTER
III

The Recruitment of Young Women to Deviant Street Networks: The Role of Domestic Networks

Among female street hustlers in Milwaukee there are three analytically distinct, although occasionally intersecting, paths that lead to involvement in deviant street networks. The first is related to membership in a particular familial network; the second stems from the vulnerable position young women find themselves in because they are runaways; and the third is the result of drug use. As is suggested by the illustrative case of Sandra, the nature and structure of familial relations often provide the motivation and at times, as in the case of Betsy, the opportunities that lead to a life of street hustling. These same relations frequently pattern street life and provide either the support and impetus necessary for successful withdrawal from the streets or make withdrawal almost impossible.

The nature and structure of familial relations seem to vary with race-ethnicity as well as with income. The effect of these variables is especially striking in shaping the initial recruitment of the young woman to the street. A particular type of familial form, the "domestic network," seems directly or indirectly responsible for the recruitment of the majority of black women who become involved in street hustling. This network consists of households linked together on the basis of kinship, pseudo-kinship, and reciprocal personal and economic relationships. It is the characteristic familial formation among poor urban blacks (Stack 1974). Specifically, it is the intersection of domestic and deviant street networks that frequently provides a direct path to the life of the streets. At the very least, it supplies a setting that allows young black women who actually reach the street via an alternate route an important up-close glimpse of hustling as a lifestyle. This chapter focuses on the role of this particular familial form in the *recruitment* of young black women to the fast life. The succeeding chapter will examine the recruitment of women via routes that do not seem to vary as much on the basis of race or income but are still influenced by the nature and structure of familial relationships: running away and drug use.

The Variability of Familial Form

It became evident early in the interviewing process that the living arrangements described by the women interviewed differed significantly by race and income in ways that had implications for their criminal behavior. Although the variety of familial forms over time and across informants was very great, generally speaking, the poorer the woman was as a child, the more likely she was to have spent most of her youth in households composed of extended family and/or non-family rather than immediate kin only. The wealthier the woman was as a child, the more likely she was to have grown up in something approaching a nuclear family with both parents present. Somewhere in between were women who had been raised in relatively isolated single-parent units.

Black women were most likely to have spent the greater part of their youths as members of shifting sets of households composed of kin, pseudo-kin, and non-kin—that is, in domestic networks. Hispanic women and the American Indian woman interviewed spent most of their childhoods in households composed of extended kin only. White women were more likely than any other group to have been raised in families that were either single-parent families that were not part of an extensive kin-based support network or nuclear families where both parents were present.

One black woman spent most of her youth in foster homes and institutions, as did one white woman.

The Path Via Domestic Networks

Since many of the women I came to know well in Milwaukee were recruited to deviant street networks through their involvement in particular domestic networks, a detailed discussion of the domestic network seems needed. It is important to note, however, that what seems to be crucial in determining whether or not a young woman takes this route is the degree of intersection between the domestic network and the deviant street network and, at times, the degree to which parents and/or guardians successfully protect their female charges from being drawn into those deviant networks. Because of the severe limitations that poverty places upon the control exercised by parents and guardians, young women from poor families are more likely to be recruited to deviant networks than are those from families that are better off. Moreover, because of the greater frequency of highly developed and far-reaching domestic networks among poor blacks than among poor whites, black girls appear to be differentially recruited to the fast life of the streets.

The Nature of Domestic Networks

Several scholars have attempted to describe the emergence and operation of the social networks that arise among the members of economically alienated segments of a highly stratified society (for example, Bott 1971; Maher 1976; Stack 1974; Suttles 1968; and Valentine 1978). Such networks appear to come into being as the result of numerous and intersecting individual attempts to achieve some semblance of financial and emotional security. This is accomplished by inducing a sense of personal indebtedness in those upon whom one would like to be able to depend. The exact methods employed to achieve this desired state vary, as do definitions of appropriate and beneficial reciprocators. The choice of method and partner, however, is clearly shaped by systems of stratification based on sex, race, and/or caste-like characteristics that coexist and crosscut the dominant class-based system.

The best study of these networks as they meet the survival needs of poor urban blacks is Carol Stack's *All Our Kin* (1974). Participants in what she was the first to call domestic networks are recruited from among one's kin and friends. Domestic networks are not visible groups because they have no obvious nucleus or defined boundary. However, a cooperative cluster of adult females is crucial since a primary focus of domestic networks is childcare arrangements (93–94).

Domestic networks are established as a result of reciprocal obligations that emerge from the swapping of goods and services over time. The particular set of individuals with whom one member of a domestic network has this sort of relationship and to whom that person may or may not be related by blood Stack refers to as "personal kindred" (44). As already alluded to above, an individual may also be drawn into a domestic network through shared rights in children. When a young woman becomes pregnant, the closest adult female kin of the woman, or of the unborn child, is expected to assume partial responsibility for the child. Thus, the father's female kin are potentially responsible for the child's welfare, as is the young woman's female kin. If a pattern of reciprocal activity develops among these possible providers and/or between them and the child, a domestic network may result. Thus, as Stack describes it:

> In the process of exchange, people become immersed in a domestic web of a large number of kinfolk who can be called upon for help and who can bring others into the network. Domestic networks comprise the network of cooperating kinsmen activated from participants' overlapping personal kindreds. Domestic networks are not ego-centered; several participants in the network can recruit kin and friends to participate in domestic exchanges. Similar to personal kindreds, domestic networks are a selection of individuals mobilized for extended periods of time (44).

Domestic networks are then often in flux. Personnel change with the ebb and flow of economic crises and opportunities, changing lifestyles, and vacillating personal relationships. Household composition and obligations are influenced by these networks. They account for where people sleep, where they eat, where their children are cared for, and where they chip in for rent, food, and other necessities or get bailed out of financial or other difficulties. For example, a sudden stroke of economic bad luck may be compensated for by means of the cash reserve of a temporarily better-off member of one's domestic network. On the one hand, then, domestic networks act as safety nets for the poor in the event of a late welfare check, robbery, sickness, or other economic disaster. On the other hand, however, they prohibit those who might, through hard work or good fortune, achieve some equity and perhaps become upwardly mobile from doing so. To disentangle oneself would mean withdrawing one's resources from the other needy souls in one's domestic network. In a world filled with possible economic setbacks, this can be a very dangerous move (Stack 1974: 90–107).

Another consequence of poverty, and the adjustment to it that is the domestic network, is a relative elasticity of residence patterns. It is not uncommon in AFDC families for a youngster to grow up in a three-generation household (Ladner 1971: 60). Even when persons move to separate households, their social, economic, and domestic lives are so entwined with other kin that they consider themselves simultaneously a part of the residential groupings of their kin. In this situation, young women who have become mothers and are old enough to receive their own AFDC checks sometimes attempt to set up separate households with or without their children, husbands, or boyfriends. Welfare regulations encourage mothers to set up separate households, as do young women's desires for privacy, independence, and a better quality of life. But these attempts can often be short-lived because of all sorts of economic or social contingencies. Although it is true that women with children have far more economic security than men and women who are not linked to welfare through a child, given the possible demands of kin and a young woman's own possible economic crises, this economic security is more of an illusion than a reality. As a result more young females with or without children remain living at home with their mothers or other adult female relatives (Stack 1974: 122). What results from failed efforts to achieve independence, however, as well as from setbacks such as evictions, fires, changes in lifestyle, and lovers' quarrels and fights is a residential pattern characterized by relatively frequent moves within a delimited geographical area and successive recombinations of household members.

The important role of the black female within these households has frequently been noted. Her relative power is surely
enhanced by the greater success of black females compared to
males in the legitimate job market and the crucial role she plays
as a link between the household and the welfare system. However,
both Stack (1974) and Joyce Ladner (1971) stress the cooperative
nature of the relationship between male and female siblings who
share the same household or live in close proximity. A jobless
male, or one working part-time or involved in seasonal labor,
often lives with his mother or, if she is dead, with his sisters and
brothers or aunts. This pattern continues even after he has established sexual relationships with women and fathered children.
Despite all the literature on the female-headed household, male
relatives, by birth or marriage, and boyfriends are almost always
around such households as members, boarders, or friends (Stack
1974: 104).

Household composition within this nation's ghettos, then,
is complex and changes relatively frequently. The physical location of households changes as well. Furthermore, both sorts of
movements are affected by and affect the exchanges and interactions that occur within domestic networks.

Domestic Networks and Deviant Street Networks: The Interface

The majority of examples of resource exchange Stack provides are of sums inherited, earned as a wage, or obtained through
welfare. She seldom hints that such sums might have been
obtained illegally. Neither does she discuss in much depth the fact
that individuals may mobilize members of their domestic network
not only to face economic and social crises and to take advantage
of legitimate opportunities but to take advantage of illegitimate
opportunities as well. As a matter of fact, this is a very common
way for youngsters to get a taste of hustling.

Bettylou Valentine argues that, in the slums and ghettos of
large American cities, "everyone beyond early childhood has
knowledge of or at least indirect contact with 'hustling' as a possible alternative source of income" (1978: 23). Reports about their
families by female street hustlers in Milwaukee confirm this
observation. Women told of fathers who were bootleggers and
mothers and brothers who "sold a little weed." They also talked

about sisters and cousins who made money by having sex with neighborhood men. "Hustling," then, refers to a wide variety of "unconventional, sometimes extralegal or illegal activities, often frowned upon by the wider community but widely accepted and practiced in the slums" (Valentine 1978: 23). It includes gambling, bootlegging, buying and selling hot goods, stripping stolen cars or abandoned buildings for anything salable, shoplifting, and selling drugs. Although some community members would object, Valentine says that others would probably also include mugging, burglary, and even armed robbery (24). On the basis of life history data gathered in Milwaukee, I would argue that one could probably add to Valentine's list purse snatching, prostitution, and pimping. However, here, too, it should be noted that many community members would not consider such activities "legitimate" hustling.

Within a particular Milwaukee household hustling activity is viewed with varying degrees of approval or disapproval dependent on a person's age, sex, economic situation, occupation, religiosity, and the activity in question. The membership of a household, then, is not seen as a pool of individuals equally ready for a hustle. Rather, the intersecting circles of personal kindred, both friends and kin, that make up the domestic network may be seen as composed of some social circles that are more prone to hustling as an economic source than others and as crosscut by another set of circles whose sole purpose is hustling. These latter are what I refer to above as deviant street networks. The fact that most of the hustling is done by young people and that males appear to do more than females makes the further specification internal to domestic networks plausible, as does the fact that so many young Milwaukee women reported hiding their hustling activities from their parents or guardians. Clear disapproval on the part of these elders for hustlers who have become prominent members of their daughters' personal kindred provides evidence of the additional set of intersecting deviant street circles. One element being interjected with this more differentiated model of a domestic network, then, is a certain internal social tension and distancing that results from the very nature of a domestic form whose existence is based at least partially on activity that is disapproved and even rejected by some of the members and on links with other social circles whose members are seen as a threat. A certain tenuous equilibrium is possible as long as economic arrangements do not lead to situations (for example, arrests, fights) that undermine social bonds.

The members of domestic networks who are more or less actively involved in hustling, then, are usually members of deviant street networks whether or not they combine their hustling with a straight job or welfare receipt. Deviant networks are linked by them to domestic networks. In other words, the social positions held by such persons are the locus of the intersection between the two sorts of networks. Especially among young adults, there is often a good deal of overlap in membership so that the ties between domestic networks and deviant street networks are often strong ones. At times the two sets of networks support each other's existence; at others they are perceived to be and are a challenge. Usually, they are curiously a little of both.

Differences among Domestic Networks, Extended Families, and Nuclear Families

Although Stack (1974) and Valentine (1978) are concerned with the situation of underclass blacks and the survival strategies they employ, I would argue that there are some limited similarities between the reality they describe and the situation of poor whites and Hispanics that stem from their shared economic status. The tendency for the dominant family form of a group to be an extended one is generally a function of survival strategies adaptive to economic stress.

Assuming that parents and/or guardians want to prevent their charges from involvement in street life and at least attempt their supervision to this end, the success of such attempts may, in part, depend on the frequency and intensity of contacts with hustlers and their world. The chances of this occurring, all other things being equal, are greater in extended family forms, especially domestic networks, than in nuclear families. This is due to the fact that extended family forms, partly because they include households in different physical sites, are by their very structure and size more permeable than the nuclear form.

White and Hispanic families under sustained economic stress will tend to extend, then. The point is that what is being described here is a continuum rather than a set of discrete categories. The crucial fact remains, however, that the domestic network as a survival strategy is clearly not as developed among poor whites or poor Hispanics as it is among impoverished blacks.

The intricate domestic network of the black underclass is not a reality for poor whites (or the majority of poor Hispanics) perhaps because the unique historical conditions for its emergence have been relatively absent; the poverty has never been as sustained or as deep, the physical segregation as rigid, the discrimination as harsh, the unemployment or underemployment as widespread, the chances for upward mobility as bleak. Another major difference is the absence, especially among poor whites, of highly developed patterns of shared rights and obligations in children. The circulation of children as a method of assuring their care, freeing mothers to bring in an income, and creating indebtedness is a crucial aspect of the domestic network among blacks. It is interestingly both a reason for its emergence and a result of its existence. In other words, the pattern has come to have a certain cultural basis in the black community that is lacking in the white and Hispanic communities.

What is much more characteristic of poor whites and Hispanics is the extended family or household. Although Rubin (1976) mentions "neighboring" as an important part of white working-class life, especially for sex-segregated socializing and occasional mutual aid, it is generally relationships with extended family that are described as the heart of working-class life (Gans 1962; Komarovsky 1967; LeMasters 1975, for example). As opposed to a domestic network, an extended family obviously has a nucleus and definite boundaries. On the one hand, it may fulfill some of the same essential economic functions as the domestic network; on the other, it is by its structure and composition less permeable than the domestic network, even if it encompasses several physical sites. Although the extended family may provide entree to deviant street networks through overlapping membership, then, its greater boundedness (with regard to both membership and the more limited dispersion of physical sites), implies that its structure, in and of itself, offers the youth that grow up within its confines more protection from recruitment to deviant street networks than the youth that live and grow up in domestic networks.

Toward the other end of the continuum, the extended family is, in turn, clearly more permeable than a nuclear family. This is not in any sense to place greater value on the nuclear form, because the other side of the coin is the crucial fact that extended family forms are in all probability the key to the economic survival of those who compose them. But it is to suggest that the forms that permit families to weather sustained economic stress may be ones that also place the youngsters within them at greater risk of being recruited to the streets. What is implied here is that on the particular dimension of permeability the domestic network typical of underclass blacks is located at one end of a continuum, whereas the nuclear family of middle-class whites is at the other. To the extent that sustained poverty causes families to extend, they move along the continuum from relatively impermeable to more permeable.

This analysis may, in turn, suggest an explanation of the greater involvement of young black women in street hustling relative to their numbers in the population than whites or Hispanics. As mentioned at the outset of this chapter, there appear to be three possible routes to the streets. Two of them, running away and drug use, are equally available to white, black, and Hispanic young women (although I will argue below that Hispanics may be slightly more apt to be drawn to the streets via drug use). The third route, that via domestic networks, however, is not likely to be taken by Hispanics and even less likely to be taken by whites. Yet it is the most frequently taken route to the streets. Young underclass black women have the dubious advantage of greater access to this route.

The Consequences of Familial Form for Recruitment to Hustling and Involvement in Deviant Street Networks

The pattern that emerges from the life histories recorded in Milwaukee indicates that nonwhites are much more likely than whites to have relatives who have been arrested for crimes. In addition, within race/ethnicity categories, blacks who resided in nuclear two-parent families seem less likely to have had relatives who have been arrested for crimes than blacks who grew up in other familial forms. I make this statement with some caution because only two black women interviewed actually grew up in nuclear families. It is also obvious that the differential sizes of the two familial forms, in and of themselves, may account for this observation: that is, the larger the familial unit, the more likely one is to have relatives who have had run-ins with the law, regardless of familial form. The same seems true of whites, however. It is interesting to note, furthermore, that seventeen (53%) of the black women who had relatives arrested had been arrested at least once for a crime committed with a relative. Sixteen of those women grew up in domestic networks. Thus, 55.2 percent of the women who grew up in domestic networks had relatives who had been arrested and had also been arrested themselves for a crime committed with a relative. This is striking when compared with similar data for whites. Although six white women (25%) had relatives who had been arrested for crimes, no white woman had ever been arrested for a crime committed with a relative. Two of the Hispanic women interviewed were sisters, lived together as children in an extended family, and had committed crimes together. They had never been arrested as the result of such activity, however, nor had they been arrested with any of their relatives who had had run-ins with the law. The American Indian woman had several siblings who had been arrested, but she had never been arrested for crimes engaged in with them.

Young black women, then, seem more likely not only to have been exposed to criminal activity as a direct result of the familial form in which they were raised than other women but also to have actually engaged in such activity as the result of relationships forged within the context of that form. Moreover, it is important to note that data presented here probably underestimate the impact of the interface between domestic and deviant street networks on the criminal behavior of such young women. First, some of the crimes young women and their relatives have committed have not resulted in arrests. Second, some of the people with whom these women have committed crimes were members of their domestic network although not relatives. Finally, very often "men" with whom they became involved and committed crimes were initially met through domestic network members but are not included here as relatives.

These findings should not be taken to suggest that there is no interaction between the members of the two racial/ethnic groups discussed here. Although poor whites may squeeze some little comfort out of the knowledge that at least they're not black (Howell 1973; LeMasters 1975), poor black, white, and Hispanic communities in Milwaukee are geographically close to one another and integrated with one another to some extent. As a result, blacks, whites, and Hispanics do become part of each other's networks. This may occur through marriage, sexual alliances, shared rights and obligations in children, or friendships that develop in the neighborhood, at school, at work, or on a hustle. It would appear, however, that, because of racism and a relative absence of domestic networks among poor whites, whites are more likely to be drawn into black domestic networks than vice versa. Hispanics seem the least likely to share domestic networks with either whites or blacks because of the isolating and insulating forces that derive from their shared ethnically based culture, the fact that they speak a language different from the majority, and the uncertain status of many with regard to permanent legal residency in the United States.

The Mechanics of Recruitment via Domestic Networks

In terms of actual recruitment via domestic networks, two variables seem to be of utmost importance. The first, the degree of intersection between domestic and deviant networks, has already been addressed. The remainder of this chapter will focus upon the second, the degree to which parents and/or guardians successfully protect their daughters from being drawn into those deviant networks.

Efforts to Protect Female Charges from Recruitment

Many of the street women in Milwaukee had started quite young to shoplift their own clothes, often with young relatives or friends, from places like Woolworth's or J. C. Penney's. Other members of their households were involved in similar activities that brought into the domestic unit items for their own use as well as items for exchange or profit. It was not unusual for women to report that other household members bought and sold marijuana or cocaine, stolen clothes or small appliances, or bootlegged liquor.

Even though others in the household might be involved in such activities, mothers and/or fathers or guardians usually reacted with disapproval to this sort of behavior on the part of their children. When elders would inquire as to where the new clothes came from, most of the informants reported that as little girls they lied. One woman who regularly shoplifted as an adult as a way of earning a living and supporting a heroin habit said that she used to tell her mother that she had swapped with a friend. A few mothers who were especially burdened with many children and had limited funds, were actively involved in hustling themselves, and/or were addicts or alcoholics would simply ignore the new acquisitions or issue a warning. One mother who discovered that her daughter had been sleeping with neighborhood boys for money simply said: "Girl, you're moving way too fast. You're gonna get your ass in some real trouble when you get eighteen." Other young women did little or no hustling on their own or in groups as juveniles even though they saw it around them. Many of these had strictly enforced curfews and were forced to attend church frequently. This pattern did not mean that these women did not become involved in deviant street networks. It did mean, however, that they did not become involved in them directly via domestic networks.

Another pattern that will be discussed in the next chapter is one that results from attempts on the part of parents or guardians to limit their daughters' interactions with negative influences in the community to a degree that is clearly far from the norm. This may have been a pattern throughout a girl's childhood or may have been initiated with the onset of puberty. In either case, one reaction to these sorts of limitations is running away, which is an alternate route to involvement in the fast life.

As opposed to involvement in deviant activity either individually or with friends as a young teen, most of the women who may be said to have taken the route via domestic networks describe first getting recruited to deviant street networks in the tenth or eleventh grades when they were about sixteen or seventeen years old. Even when this activity did begin to be engaged in on a regular basis, however, again it was usually kept from elders for as long as possible. Many parents and guardians only found out or had their suspicions confirmed at the time of the young girl's first contact with the police or even her first arrest and confinement in jail.

In short, recruiters were rarely those directly supervising these young women. Even when parents or guardians were actively involved in hustling themselves, their disapproval as well as a certain age-grading and specialization within deviant networks generally prevented parents and guardians from being in the same networks. Rather, recruiters were older siblings or stepsiblings, cousins, or young aunts or uncles or the personal kindred or friends of these relatives. It is important to note that slightly older domestic network members who were also deviant street network members sometimes did not encourage young women to get involved in the fast life, however, and, indeed, at times are reported to have discouraged it.

Especially older kin or fictive kin who, for whatever reason, were seen by themselves and by the potential recruit as at least informal guardians appear to have acted on occasion as gatekeepers with regard to the entry of a young woman into a deviant network. A girl who appears, then, through word and action to be even fleetingly interested in becoming a part of a deviant network may be encouraged or discouraged. This seems to be dependent on her prior relationship with the potential recruiter, the commitment of the girl to becoming involved, and the perceptions of the gatekeeper with regard to how inevitable it is that she will at some time live the fast life, how appropriate the intended activity is thought to be for women in general and for her in particular, the risk of the intended activity to her person and her future, and how much of an asset or debit to the enterprise under consideration she will be. Because of such reservations, young women often appear to be recruited by people who are less likely to have such reservations because they are marginal or newly recruited to the domestic network themselves. Recruitment by both kin and more marginal domestic network members occurs, however.

Parents and formal (but not necessarily legal) guardians I spoke with and observed were overwhelminly opposed to the fast life for their children no matter what their race and stressed the merits of education as the key to economic success. Female street hustlers also generally reported that this was the message they had received throughout childhood. Moreover, this was the case even when they themselves were currently, or had been at one time, engaged in some form of street hustling. Rather, the permeability of the domestic network as compared to the extended or nuclear family is, I believe, an important reason why black women take this route more often than white. No matter to what lengths parents and guardians go to keep their children untainted by street life, the greater boundedness of the extended and nuclear family seems to provide greater protection. As mentioned above, the very system that may be responsible for household survival, then, may promote the initiation of young adults into a generally disapproved way of life simply by exposing them to more possible recruiters to deviant street networks. A very striking example of this has to do with the cultural pattern of "child-keeping" described above. On the one hand, this pattern clearly promotes the care and nurturing of children in an environment of scarce and uncertain resources. Children can be shifted from household to household depending on the current circumstances of the members of a particular network. On the other hand, this pattern may maximize the exposure of children to deviant networks. Within this system, then, whether little protection from the influence of possible recruiters or an abundance of protection can be offered by parents or guardians is one of the key factors in determining the chances a young woman has of being recruited via her own domestic network.

First Hustling Experience

Often the initial recruitment as well as recruitment thereafter is described by women as rather low-key and offhand. Just as someone might approach a group chatting in a kitchen to ask for help in moving a newly acquired couch into an apartment in exchange for a beer or simply as a gesture of friendship, so might someone be asked to help lug copper tubing pilfered from an abandoned building in exchange for a share of the profits or to help sell some stolen merchandise or some marijuana in exchange for a portion of what was being sold. Furthermore, to be asked to participate in something that is forbidden to children and might be risky was often taken as affirmation of adult status and competence. This was true even if a young woman realized, as one informant did, that her brother just needed her to help him cash a stolen check because the payee was a female and he needed the money quickly to make a drug deal. When he observed that she did not get flustered when he took her to a tavern to cash the check, he offered to teach her how to make money "passing paper." He showed her how to recognize income tax refund checks through the slits in mailboxes and how to pop the locks on those that had been so secured. He explained to her that this work was only seasonal, but that these checks were easier to cash than welfare checks. Although welfare checks were easier to come by, most welfare recipients had neighborhood people who routinely cashed their welfare checks. Most of the people who would cash a welfare check in the community, then, were suspicious of new faces or checks payable to women with unfamiliar names. When a friend of this brother's needed an accomplice in a credit card fraud, the fellow volunteered his sister.

In this fashion, deviant street networks develop, and, after having been passively recruited, the young woman herself may recruit a sister or friend to engage in the newly learned activity. When I met this particular woman, she had just been released from prison for forging a series of checks issued by the U.S. Department of the Treasury (Internal Revenue Service). Her brother and his girlfriend had been convicted of the same offense.

Childbirth as a Turning Point in Recruitment

Although many of the informants had done some freelance hustling in their early teens, getting actively involved in a deviant street network implies engaging in a variety of hustling ventures, usually with others, on a fairly regular basis. It rests on one's ability to organize one's life, at least for a while, around hustling. This takes a degree of time and freedom that very young teenagers usually do not have. Moreover, it involves a redefinition of self that is usually not easy for someone who is being defined by her status as a high school student as well as by her significant others as still a child.

This pattern tended to occur, then, slightly later in these girls' lives, often after the birth of a first child. This event was particularly important because, for many of the women, it meant both an actual and a symbolic change in status. Symbolically, as Ladner points out early in her study of black adolescent girls in St. Louis: "If there was one common standard for becoming a woman that was accepted by the majority of the people in the community, it was the time when girls gave birth to their first child. This line of demarcation was extremely clear and separated the *girls* from the *women*" (1971: 212).

The importance of this event for the entry, especially of young black women, into deviant street networks is that it lessened the legitimacy of rules advanced by parents and guardians who tried to set limits on the activities of these young women. Efforts at social control were, thus, to a certain degree, automatically undermined.

In actuality, depending on the girl's age, the event also meant that she was eligible to collect her own AFDC check. This often allowed her to get her own apartment. Another possibility is that she would move in with the father of her child or a current lover whether or not she was still a minor. Thus, she was also able to be physically distant from the sources of external control.

At this point the young woman is in a very vulnerable position because of the loosened ties to parents and/or guardians and because her welfare check or the income provided by her lover, it soon becomes clear, is not the key to independence she may have thought it was. She may be having a hard time making it financially and may be feeling a bit tied down at a time when she expected to feel for the first time a measure of independence. This may be true even if, as was often the case among informants, she is getting a great deal of help with childcare from her mother or other female relatives.

It is at this time that the Milwaukee street hustlers I came to know seemed especially likely to get really involved in the fast life. Even if the welfare money was being collected by the guardians or mothers of these women because of their status as minors and they were not able, alone or with a lover, to get their own apartments, the symbolic content of this event seemed to loosen controls to an unprecedented degree and was followed by a greater measure of illicit behavior within the context of a deviant street network than was engaged in previously. If the pregnancy meant, as it did for most, that the young woman dropped out of high school and did not return, it also meant that that source of self-definition and day-to-day involvement as a juvenile was also suddenly absent. Such women often tried to get straight jobs, but soon found, if they had not discovered it before the pregnancy, that the street had more to offer in terms of ready cash, independence, and excitement (as well as risks) than the dead-end jobs they could land. As Mildred, a woman who after having a miscarriage returned to school at her mother's insistence only to graduate four months pregnant, said:

I thought by graduating everything was gonna be okay, you know, 'cause that's what they tell me, you know, 'cause, like, I got a high school diploma; hey, I made it. I'm a free woman; I'm of age, you know; come on here. I had a son to support, you know. I had to make money even quicker. I don't know if they looked at it that way. Um, I just figured, God, I'm never gonna be able to get a job. Then the job they was offerin' me . . . oh, I can't work for this less money. You got to be crazy, I said. There's a faster way out there. I worked for a dollar sixty-seven from February to April, a dollar sixty-seven at Marc's Big Boy [a fast food chain], and I think that was really against my constitutional rights. But I didn't have no choice. I need a job and I grab it. And I thought: "I'm not gonna work for a dollar sixty-seven; I'm not! I told 'em . . . I said: "Damn. This is nineteen seventy-nine. What is this here?" It was a trip. They don't know what they doin' to these young women with their job 'cause . . . it don't make 'em working' any harder; it don't. It makes 'em want to get it faster. You might meet somebody you're waitin' on one day, gives you a wink and telephone number . . . or come on up to his apartment, or: "I got a better position for you upstairs." I did.

It is important to note that many young mothers in this situation do, indeed, settle down at a straight job and/or continue in school. Several factors may facilitate this outcome. Although I had little contact with young women from this same community who were straight, one can hypothesize that again the degree of intersection between the girl's domestic network or household and deviant street networks and the ability of her parents or guardians to protect her from negative community influences, as well as her own assessment of her potential based on her past performance in school and/or the quality of her first job certainly are important variables. I would also venture to say that there is a certain amount of chance involved. Even though the women I spent most of my time with had opted for the streets, some of them did have straight siblings, step-siblings, and other relatives. One woman, Diane, who had five siblings and step-siblings and whose mother had been in Taycheedah when the children were young described a family joke that centered on such a situation:

When I was little, I lived with my mother's legal guardian. Four of us lived with her. The two youngest stayed with our grandmother. All of us except for one child has been in trouble with the law. My sister was in Taycheedah; my brother was in Waupun . . . all of us was in jail around the same time. The only one that didn't get in any trouble was my little sister. She's the balanced one in my family. She's twenty now. She's so upstanding. Do you think she'd get in trouble? She wouldn't do anything. Like all of us, my mother and me like to smoke a little weed now and then. And my little sister, she don't even smoke cigarettes, let alone weed. She also don't drink . . . like when I was pregnant, oh, she used to put up with me. I was terrible. She would never get pregnant 'til she got married. There's a joke in our family that they brought the wrong baby home from the hospital.

It is obviously possible for young women who are unmarried to have a first child and become more settled because of it. It is also possible for sisters to react differently to having a child themselves or to the idea of having a child (one must not forget that two sisters may, and often do, have different domestic networks and that this is especially likely if there is a great deal of difference in their ages). The important point to be made here is that the birth of the first child often did seem to be a turning point in the lives of Milwaukee's female street hustlers.

The recruitment of one particular informant illustrates very well how the birth of the first child may loosen parental controls. It also highlights the importance of the intersection of domestic and deviant street networks. Loretta was one of ten children. She was twenty-seven when I met her and had been an active street hustler for eight years. She had no juvenile record although she does recall being truant from school. Her mother died when she was fourteen, and her father was caring for the family. She complains that he was grumpy and didn't approve of any of his daughter's boyfriends. She says of this period in her life:

I was just missin' school, you know, tryin' to pass on just once a week, get my subjects done. . . . I would always go to my morning class but then after lunch . . . that was play-

around time, especially if it was a class I didn't like. I was
missin' school and doin' everythin'. Daddy used to tell me,
particularly on Sunday: "Don't play hooky anymore." Particularly on Sunday he'd tell me I couldn't go to the basketball game. And when it was my birthday, I went, you know.
My birthday was always around the time of a basketball
tournament. And I went. And he couldn't stop me. So I
decided after a while what I was gonna do . . . I wanted to
get pregnant. I didn't just get pregnant. I wanted to get
pregnant to settle down.

Loretta transferred to a school for pregnant high school
students shortly after her son was born. It was her mother's dying
wish that her children should stay in school until they graduated.
Loretta graduated, got on welfare, and moved out:

I moved on my own. And I took care of my son, got on
welfare and then when I saw he wuz gettin' older and me
and my family, daddy and them wuz comin' back closer
together . . . 'cause they all wuz upset 'cause I moved
. . . then eventually I decided I would look for me a job, and
I found a job, and I got the lady to keep him that used to live
in the projects with us before we moved. She kept him, and I
paid her while I worked. I wuz workin' second shift. And
then eventually I met this guy that wanted to be a pimp.
That's how this all started. I met him. He had got out of the
House of Correction from being there two years for driver's
. . . revocation of his license or something . . . and, uh,
okay, my cousin was already going with his brother ["going
with" implies he was her pimp], and my oldest brother told
him about me along with the guy's brother that went with
my cousin. And, so, when the guy come out, he come to my
house 'cause me and my cousin wuz tight, and I eventually
started goin' with him. I ended up being his prostitute,
whorin' for him. . . . He had been into burglary and other
things before. He had never pimped, but he wanted him
some whores.

When I met Loretta, she had just finished serving time for
knifing to death a woman she had been in a fight with. During

her career on the streets she had been a prostitute, carried a concealed weapon and trafficked in weapons, recruited other women
to work as prostitutes for her "man" (to be her wives-in-law),
stolen cars, sold drugs, and been a pickpocket, a till-tapper
(someone who learns to deftly take money from an open cash
register while an accomplice distracts the cashier), a robber, and
an embezzler. She sometimes had straight jobs during this time,
and she continued to collect welfare during much of this period.
Even when she was on the run from local authorities, she continued to send money to her father and sisters for their support
and the support of her son. Loretta's story is typical in every way
but one. She claims to have deliberately planned her first pregnancy. No other informant claimed to have done that, and I have
reason to suspect that even her pregnancy was not as planned as
she suggests. Loretta is also older than most of the women I came
to know. She is probably near the end of her career as a street
hustler. She is too old to be marketable on the streets as a prostitute and further arrests would carry severe penalties for her.

For young women who are recruited into deviant street networks as Loretta was, involvement in hustling may come to be
just one of the ways in which they contribute to their own support, the support of their children, and the well-being of their
domestic network or extended family or household. Here, acquir-
ing money, goods, and services by means of a hustle may simply
be a part of everyday living.

CHAPTER
IV
Running Away and Drug Use as Routes to Deviant Networks

To the degree that intersecting familial and street networks are present, a woman's chances of living a predominantly straight or fast life are facilitated or retarded. Crosscutting the family-structure variable, however, is another equally potent variable: conflict with familial authority. Family conflict negatively affects the ability of parents and/or guardians to control the behavior of young women in their charge and protect them from being recruited to street life. As used here, this variable is a socio-emotional one and has to do with the quality of the attachment between the young woman and the household members who have authority over her. To the degree that conflict between the young women and/or their legal or informal guardians leads to an attenuation or complete undermining of this attachment and the authority that is based on it, young women are vulnerable to recruitment to the streets. It is this dimension that appears correlated with the second and third routes to the street briefly touched on in the last chapter: running away and drug use.

Running Away

A national survey of runaways indicates that in 1975 about 733,000 youths ran away. For the purposes of that study a runaway was defined as a youth ten to seventeen years old who was absent at least overnight without parental permission. The study also indicated that about half of the runaways that year were girls (47%); that runaways were more likely to come from low-income families than from the middle or upper part of the income distribution (the rate was about 40 percent higher for adolescents from low-income families); that racial differences in running away were slight (white, 2.9%; black, 3.2%; and Hispanic, 4.6%); that households having two members, usually a parent and a child, were much more likely (5.1%) to have a child run away than households having four persons (1.9%); and that the highest rate (7.1%) occurred in households of eight or more persons (Opinion Research Corporation 1976).

Tim Brennan, David Huizinga, and Delbert Elliott have, through multivariate analysis, generated a typology of runaways (Brennan 1980: 198–203). They feel that there are two general classes of runaways. Class I is defined as not highly delinquent and, in general, not alienated from family and school. The members of this category tend to have, on balance, positive motivations for running away including a desire to explore, to meet new people, and to have new experiences. They do not appear to be very different from non-runaways in terms of alienation from parents or school nor do they appear to be more delinquent. The literature in this area seems to suggest that about one-fifth of runaways are of this type (Brennan et al. 1978; Libertoff 1980; Walker 1975; Wattenberg 1956). Class II runaways are characterized as "delinquent" and "alienated" (Brennan 1980: 200). Although there are several types within each class, generally speaking, this second category includes two groups. First, there are those adolescents who are obviously alienated from school, feel parental control is too restrictive, have had quarrels with parents or teachers, and have been involved in a variety of delinquent activities alone or with peers. This group is usually thought to be the largest category, accounting for perhaps 75 percent of the total (Nye 1980: 5). Second, there are what have come to be called in the literature "pushouts." These youngsters have been abandoned or told to leave by parents. There are no exact estimates of the size of this group, but it may be about 5 percent of the total (Butler et al. 1974).

Most runaways do not run far or stay long. The national survey referred to above found that 20 percent traveled less than a mile and 52 percent less than ten miles. Only 18 percent traveled farther than fifty miles. Forty percent had returned within a week, 84 percent were back within a month, 9 percent were gone up to six months, and 5 percent had not returned at the time the national survey was taken (Opinion Research Corporation 1976). Many runaways who cannot or do not want to live at home find life in the streets no better and alternate between returning home and going back to the streets (Nye 1980: 5).

About half of the female street hustlers I obtained life histories from describe running away from home as an event critical to their recruitment to street life. These women fall into three groups: a very small group of women from stable working-class and middle-class households who seem to have been provided with substantial financial and emotional support by their parents and/or guardians; women who are totally bereft of resources and who really have been forced to run away from home or the institutions in which they were confined, because they were abused or unwanted; and women from stable, if poor, households embedded in domestic networks that overlap with deviant street networks who have had major conflicts with those who are their immediate caretakers. The first group of women tended to have fewer kin or fictive kin who made a living as part of deviant street networks and more siblings and step-siblings who earned an income exclusively or almost exclusively from a straight job. They were also more often clearly suburban in origin. The second group can only be characterized as pushouts. The third group is a distinct subcategory of women whose domestic networks interface with deviant street networks. They were recruited to the streets as a result of their contact with deviant street networks, but only after the relationship with the primary caretaker was undermined.

The recruitment to street life of runaways appeared to be similar for blacks and whites. All of the women who were recruited to deviant street networks by this route would be categorized as delinquent and alienated (Brennan et al. 1978). Although Brennan and his collaborators indicate that most pushouts are boys from lower-class families, some of these women clearly had no choice but to leave their households. They tended to come

from desperately poor households that were often headed by or
contained alcoholics, drug addicts, and/or persons who had
serious and repeated run-ins with the law. Most of the other
members of these households (and membership tended to shift
frequently) were involved in street life, and the household itself
tended to occupy a sort of pariah status in the community. These
women were also more likely than others to report having been
sexually and/or physically abused as children. It is quite possible
that they were from households that were at one time part of an
intricate domestic network as described in the prior chapter, but
that, for one reason or another, no longer were, since their caretakers had been unable to sustain the reciprocity upon which
membership in such networks depends.

Women who enter street life by running away, then, are
from families that offer their young women a good deal of emotional support as well as from households so fraught with economic, legal, social, and emotional difficulty that, when the
young women leave, they are barely missed. As will be shown
below, the parents and/or guardians in the first category often
seem to have overreacted to signs of deviance or impending
deviance on the parts of their female charges, while parents
and/or guardians in the second category seem to have hardly
reacted at all.

Runaways with Resources

There is a surprising consistency in the themes of the stories
women tell about the situations that precipitated their leaving
home. Many felt that, for one reason or another, they were singled
out among their siblings and step-siblings for especially favorable
or unfavorable treatment. In many cases there is reason to believe
that this may have been so because they were the only children
mothers had had by men other than the men who fathered the rest
of their children, for example, or because they strikingly
resembled lovers of their mothers' whom the mothers would
rather have forgotten.

One woman felt that she was clearly her parents' "pick" and
that that status caused her brothers and sisters to treat her badly as
a result of their jealousy. More typical is the following statement:

When I was little, I was always the one that was odd. I
always did things. My mother said that I was "black-
hearted" and that I was "evil." And she told me that constantly. And they used to call me "blackie" and "darkie." I
was very insulted and sensitive. I got my feelings hurt and
always ran to my father for comfort and my grandmother.

Those women who were neither pushouts nor domestic
network members, even if they did not feel they had been chosen,
for whatever reason, to be recipients of some uniquely negative
treatment throughout childhood, felt that, especially with the
onset of puberty, their activities were restricted in a way that their
siblings' or step-siblings' or peers' were not. In most instances the
restrictions described were put into effect when parents and/or
guardians perceived that their female charges had probably
become or were likely to become sexually active. According to my
informants, these perceptions were often inaccurate either
because the young women were not sexually active or because
they had been sexually active for some time. No matter what the
nature of the misperception, its inaccuracy seemed to alienate
these young women further. They seemed to feel indignant that
people who knew so little about their behavior in this area should
attempt to control it. Poor performance in school and/or generally disruptive activity in school including tardiness, drug use,
fighting, and truancy were also seen as meriting increased control
of young female charges.

Jeanne's description of her relationship with her parents
from about junior high on illustrates this pattern. When I met
Jeanne, she was twenty-four years old, married, and the mother of
three children, the first of which had been put up for adoption.
She was waiting to be picked up by the police for some recent
forgeries and was quite certain that she would be sentenced for a
rather lengthy period to Taycheedah. She had a history of status
offenses as a juvenile and as an adult had been involved in shoplifting and forgery on her own and in fencing stolen property and
credit card fraud with her husband and friends of his. She describes her conflicts with her parents this way:

I had a happy childhood up to the age of about fifteen.
When I was growing up, I always had nice things: nice

clothes, nice house. My parents, they give me a lot, you
know, just about whatever I wanted before I started getting
in trouble. Then I started having problems. That's when it
all started, after I was fifteen. Then I started wanting to do a
few things, and my parents just didn't seem to understand,
but now, or I should say when my brother was born, they're
a lot more lenient on him. They let him do a lot than they
ever let me do. But I think they kinda learned off me, too,
and they seen what happened to me. My parents were just
totally against Dave [the young man who was to become her
husband]. That's what it was there, you know. And, well,
my father is a real stinker and, you know, school and report
cards . . . and if I got a C or D in somethin', you know I was
grounded. I was grounded half my life with him. Every little
thing, you know: "You're grounded."

Did you skip a lot of school?

No, well, yeah, a little bit. When, you know, I got in ninth,
tenth grade, I started, you know, going outside for lunch,
and friends would come up in their cars and say: "Come on,
Jeanne let's go." Okay. It didn't take much to talk me into
somethin'. They put me away in detention a coupla times
for a coupla weeks at a time because they considered me
uncontrollable and because they didn't like Dave. And, you
know, every time they'd catch me at lunch hour at
McDonald's or somethin', they'd have the police pick me up
at night and take me away. So, then, I ran away from home.
Dave came with me. We were gone, like five months. We
stayed a coupla places and then at my cousin's. We were
dealing a lot of drugs and stuff. I was pregnant when they
caught us. They put me in Roselyn Manor [a home for
pregnant, unwed teenage girls] and then that baby they
made me give up for adoption. Then my father said I could
come back if I wouldn', you know, do all these things. And I
was not allowed to see Dave again. I said: "No way." So I
went to live with my mother's sister until I turned eighteen.
Then I married Dave.

Why didn't they like him?

Because he was, well, at first, I don't know, they just didn't like him and then he went to Wales [Ethan Allen School for Boys in Wales, Wisconsin] for car theft, he and a buncha guys from school. They just felt he wasn't the type of person I should be with. Maybe they were right in a way. But they were too strict, you know. My friends could go out 'til, you know, ten or eleven at night, you know. I had to, you know, be home at eight or nine, you know. And I just wanted to do things, not that I was doin' wrong things out there, just that they were really strict. And you just can't tell somebody they can't see somebody 'cause if you do, they're gonna see them anyhow. If you care about a person, just because your mother and father say: "Don't go see him". . . you're gonna sneak and go. It would have been a lot easier if they would have just accepted the fact.

Marilyn is a young black woman of twenty-four, the same age as Jeanne, who is white. She also describes growing up in a home in which she wanted for little. Her parents owned a house in a lower-middle-class black neighborhood in Milwaukee. Both of her parents were semi-skilled factory workers when she was growing up. She had two younger siblings, neither of whom had any trouble with the law. She describes her family situation during her childhood as one in which there was much love and a good deal of shared leisure activity. She did well in school and her friends were generally good students. Although her parents had dreams of Marilyn's going to college, at sixteen she ran away and, not too long after that, was working as a prostitute. She describes this period as follows:

The first time I caught a case I was twenty years old and that was for prostitution. I got into prostitution . . . it goes way back to when I graduated from high school. Well, my senior year in high school I ran away from home. My parents had gotten real strict and I couldn't understand it. I never had any trouble at home until my last year. My parents were really lenient with me until then. I guess they thought I was going to get pregnant or something because that's what my mother would say. "You're going to be the first one to get pregnant." That kind of made me feel bad, as if they didn't trust me. They trusted me all the way to my senior year and then I don't know what happened; they lost their trust or maybe they were just afraid I would get pregnant and not graduate and go to college. That was a big thing in our house—for me to graduate and go to college. They were pushing me too hard. Anyway, I ran away.

Where did you go?

I went over to my girlfriend's house and I just must have got really drunk 'cause I woke the next day and I had such a terrible hangover. And when I got back to the house, my parents called the police. They took me to the detention home. While I was there, I started a suit against my parents. I wanted my own custody. I was working. They said if I came home, they wouldn't be so strict.

Where did you get the idea to bring suit against your parents?

I read in the papers around this time that somebody else was doing it. It sounded good at the time, but I don't know about that. It kinda hurt my parents. Anyway, my graduation night I went to this club . . . now what's the name? Big Pip and the Cheetahs played there. Do you know the club I'm talking about?

[I suggest the name of a club on North Avenue where many hustlers hang out.]

No. Well, I went to that club and I met him [her "man"] in the bar. There was me and two other girls, and he asked us if he could buy us a drink. Then he asked us if we wanted to go to an "afterhours" and we went. We didn't have anything else to do and it was graduation night. And so he bought us a coupla drinks. And then he pulled me aside and asked me if I wanted to snort coke. And I said: "Why not?" He asked me if I wanted to go home with him and I said: "I really don't know yet." So, he sat down and talked to me, and he seemed to care, so I went home with him. And that's how I met him. We didn't have sex that night at all. I stayed with him for a month. I didn't work. I thought it was just a straight relationship. I didn't know what he did. I liked him right off the bat. So that's how I stayed with him. After a while he asked me how I would like to dance [go-go dance]. I said I would. I didn't know that along with the dancing came the hooking. The first time I went I just stripped and danced, and when I got back, did I get beat 'cause I didn't turn tricks on the side. But nobody told me that, that I was supposed to. So I continued to dance and that's when I started turning tricks.

At twenty-four, Marilyn had had cases for prostitution, forgery, credit card fraud, absconding, and various drug-related offenses. She had a fairly serious heroin addiction and had just had her probation revoked because of her involvement in an attempted forgery. One might ask why, given that she obviously came from a caring home, Marilyn did not return there after the initial beating. Apart from the fact that her "man" would probably try his best to threaten or cajole her into remaining with him, it would be, on some level, even more difficult for Marilyn to return to a home such as hers than for a similarly situated young woman to return to a household with deviant street network connections. The degree of condemnation, stigma, and guilt on the part of both the caretakers and the young woman are likely to be greater here than they would be for a young woman from a household whose membership overlaps with deviant street network membership.

In both instances just described, the parents of the young women were so alarmed and angered by their daughters' behavior that they not only requested police intervention but also permitted their daughters to be taken into custody. Other parents and/or guardians actually petitioned the juvenile court to have their daughters adjudicated delinquent for being "uncontrollable" and sent to a juvenile home. It is important to note that this action coincided with their daughters' coming to sexual maturity and their own inability to deal realistically with this fact, on the one hand, and their justified concerns about the effect of pregnancy on their daughters' ability to pursue careers goals, on the other. Their daughters' offenses up to this point had been limited to status offenses. They were known to be truant occasionally, to drink occasionally, to have associated with young men who were considered undesirable companions, and to have run away. Self-respect studies indicate that such behavior is not at all unusual for adolescents of both sexes, most of whom do not go on to live lives of crime.[1] In each case, parents and/or guardians only suspected that their daughters had become sexually active. These women were placed in detention merely "to scare them," but what happened there was truly unanticipated. Those women who had been put in detention for running away and later became involved in deviant street activities often also ran away from the detention homes, sometimes with newly acquired, streetwise friends. In these cases, it was not long before they had met a "man" and begun to hustle, usually as prostitutes.

Other parents, with even more resources at their disposal than the two described, looked to the professional expertise of religious leaders, social workers, and psychiatrists. This was true in Ruby's case. Ruby, who was twenty-five when I met her, had a long record for prostitution, forgery, theft, and drug-related offenses and had been involved in burglaries and fencing stolen merchandise. She had dropped out of high school at sixteen. She had two younger sisters, both of whom had graduated from college, married, and had children. Her father was a stockbroker and her mother an occupational therapist. She came from a wealthy suburb north of Milwaukee. When she dropped out of school, she became involved with people on the fringes of the anti-war movement. This was about 1970. She was not sexually active at the time and had had no contact with the police. Her involvement in the anti-war movement seems to have been confined to marches on the state capital and to have been motivated more by the marijuana smoking and partying that often followed such events than by any real commitment to peace. She says of this time:

> I gave my parents hell. They didn't know where I was. They always used to come down and try and find me. Then I got real scared because some friends called me to the car 'cause

1. See Cernkovich and Giordano (1979) for an excellent review of the relevant literature on this point and a discussion of their own findings.

they said he [Ruby's father] was going to take me to juvcy home. And I didn't want to go. Some of the psychiatrists we were talking to told them to leave me alone. If they tried to stop me, I probably really would have run all the further, which I agreed with. . . . I went to California and back, just partied mainly.

Upon her return to Wisconsin, Ruby's parents again consulted with a psychiatrist, helped Ruby get a job, and subsidized her purchase of a car. Shortly after that, she had a near-fatal automobile accident following two days of doing "speed" (amphetamines). When she recovered, her parents sent her to a Bible academy in South Dakota to complete high school. After graduation, she returned to Wisconsin and enrolled in a community college north of Milwaukee where she began a program of study in optical dispensing. Within six months she had tired of school and had begun to come into Milwaukee proper to "run around." Although she still had her room in the dorm, she had moved in with a young black male in the city. Nobody knew where she was. The young man "turned her out" and soon she was making a steady income as a prostitute. She says:

He told me how to go out there and get money and stuff. So I, like, went out, and, you could say, turned tricks. I never really walked the stroll 'cause he knew enough old dudes, you know. We'd go by their house or have them come to where we were staying. All this time my dad was going crazy.

Her perception of her family growing up is of a conservative backwater attempting to resist a progressive liberal tide. She refers to her parents as "Archie and Edith Bunker." They appear to have been very religious people who were upwardly mobile. Hers was a revolt not so much against a restrictive environment, then, although it was that, but against a set of values. In addition to consulting psychiatrists, Ruby's distraught parents also relied heavily on the advice of their Lutheran minister, who was a close family friend. They refused to grant the newly acquired values she was testing out any validity and met that testing alternately with psychiatric intervention, religious counseling, financial concessions, and anger and embarrassment. Although Ruby was unique among the women I came to know in terms of her background and the response of her parents to her running away, it is interesting that their efforts were no more successful than those of the less well-off parents of Jeanne and Marilyn.

At this point, it is important to mention that some of the categories into which women have been classified for the purposes of discussion in this chapter and the last were constructed more as heuristic devices than as a reflection of any true accounting. That is, some women have so many forces pushing them into "the life" that choosing among them is sometimes difficult even if a dominant one can be determined. This is not the case in this instance. The women whose cases fall into the category "runaway with resources" are really quite distinct from other women interviewed. Any variability within the category is due exclusively to my estimate of the extent of family resources. Income differences, in turn, influence what sorts of measures families take in their attempt to prevent their daughters from deviating. Only four women clearly fall into this category; three are white and one is black.

Runaways without Resources: Pushouts

The second group of young women who became involved in deviant street networks by running away are women who came from households that were terribly poor. Often the head of the household and some of the siblings or step-siblings were alcoholics, drug addicts, and/or repeatedly incarcerated. Nearly everyone in the household was attempting to make it on a hustle. The head of the household and, very occasionally, the young woman herself, was receiving some form of welfare benefits. These households were often known to the police and to their neighbors for the deviant behavior of their members. Although I can only speculate about this point, as suggested above, it appears that some of these households may once have been part of a domestic network, but were dropped because they were unable to reciprocate and were probably too much of a drain on network resources as well.

The fastest way to be dropped from one or several of the crucial reciprocal relationships that form the basis of domestic networks is to fail repeatedly to reciprocate or to be outright exploitative of the other partners. One reason why a household

might be in such a position is because the delicate balance among
the sources of income has been upset. This, in turn, may challenge the norms that govern who may participate in which
income-producing activities and result in serious dissension
within the household, especially between generations. This situation would seem to be more likely to occur when a household has
within it an addict with a very serious habit and/or people
engaged in fairly serious criminal activity. Supporting both a
habit and expensive legal fees can put a household that is already
very poor into dire economic straits. Moreover, given that women
with shared obligations for children form a crucial part of domestic networks, an addicted or alcoholic female head of household
may be disqualified from participation in a reciprocal relationship because of an inability to care for children.

In addition, as Marsha Rosenbaum points out (1981: 78),
most addicts from time to time rip off their loved ones. Even if the
female head of household is not an addict, then, if she is often
either giving other members of the household money for drugs
when she sees them getting "sick" or being ripped off for same,
she is not going to be a very reliable reciprocator.

It is clear to me as a result of my fieldwork in Milwaukee
that many households with an alcoholic or addicted member are
unable to fulfill their reciprocal obligations most of the time.
There is a certain amount of understanding within ghetto communities for such situations because of the frequency with which
they occur. If they are dropped from a network, it is less often for
moral reasons than because of the level of demand placed on the
household by the addicted or criminal member (and, perhaps, his
or her friends), the number of such members, and the resources,
legitimate and otherwise, of the other members. Obviously, there
are other disastrous situations, natural and human, that can prevent a household, or crucial members of it, from fulfilling their
obligations. My informants, however, suggest that drug addiction
and the chaotic lifestyle associated with it is a particularly important factor.

The degree of social disorganization that characterizes the
households from which pushouts come can be incredible. Even
the bonds that connect the household members to each other are,
at times, so tenuous that members relate to each other suspi-
ciously, hostilely, manipulatively, and exploitatively. One black
woman says:

I was very nice to my family. I had put them in a situation
when I was making money [as a prostitute] and didn't have
a "man." When they go to jail, all they can depend on is me,
and I come to them and I help them. I know how it feels like
being in jail. But they don't show appreciation. Every time
I'm in jail, I cannot call them . . . and say: "Help me."
They won't. The only time they so nice to me is when I'm
turning them on [providing them with drugs], you know.
Other than that we fuss and damn near kill each other, you
know. I'm not gonna stand for them hitting me no more.
My brothers are too husky and big for me to pick on. I feel
it's a shame how . . . I don't think brothers and sisters suppose to fight like that. So, I always walk out of the house
and leave there . . . until I come back. And every time I
come back, I'm turning them on again. I think they got it in
their mind where I'm suppose to take care of them. I think
that's the way they feel about me. But they don't care
nothin' about me when it comes down to it. I have to get
away from my family in order for me to go straight and on
to something else.

Another woman, Carol, who is white and resembles Ruby in
that major conflicts, especially with her father, concerning matters of political and social views contributed to her running away,
says:

Why did I run away? I don't know. I was the only
girl. . . . My father was kinda an alcoholic and there wasn't
always anything in the house to eat . . . and he was fightin'
with my ma. . . . I was the only girl and there were five
boys. There was a baby girl, but she was much younger. It
was kinda hard for me at home with all those boys. It
seemed everyone had been pickin' on me: my mother, the
kids at school. And the neighborhood guys wouldn't go out
with me because I wouldn't go to bed with them. It was just
a bad day. I said I was goin' to the gas station for a soda and
my ma said: "Be home in time for dinner." I said: "Ya," but
I never made it.

Finally, Mabel, a retired street hustler, says:

I lived in the inner core [ghetto] for approximately five years. The first four years that I remember my mother was a healthy, normal mother. She was real affectionate. She took up a lotta time with me. Then, she became bedridden [Mabel's mother had been shot in the back by a former "man" and paralyzed]. It was after that that I started takin' off. I had to start washin', ironin', takin' care of my little brothers. I wasn't allowed to go to school. I had the type of relatives that . . . they weren't that helpful, you know. They really didn't care about my mother or her kids. My older brother, she left him with somebody and they never gave him back, so he was no help. So, I ran and kept on running.

These women are more likely than other women interviewed to have been involved in violent crimes against household members, lovers, their "men," or their own children. They are also often heavy drug users. Some of them are clearly mentally ill and/or retarded. Several of the women I spoke to seem to have had such terrible childhoods that they have only confused memories of them. In describing her childhood chronologically, for example, Mabel said at one point:

Mrs. Velma, my social worker, thought maybe I was going mentally ill and emotionally ill 'cause most of my life I've always been emotionally ill. At least that's what they told me, and, um, between the ages of seven and nine, I have like a lotta blanks because they were putting me in the nut house. I think they were druggin' me. They put me in with the adults. They finally barred me from the children's part 'cause I was just too nutty.

It is interesting to note that Mabel is still selling drugs on the side although her major current role is that of college student. Her own drug use continues to be sporadically quite heavy. Her last major conviction was for conduct regardless of life (she dragged a drunk "man" from a tavern and placed him in the street, where he was repeatedly run over by passing cars). Her oldest daughter is a very active street hustler and her youngest, at the time of the interview, was in the children's section of the county mental health facility.

Vernetta is another woman who is confused about her childhood. I first spoke with her in a halfway house when she was twenty-two. She is black and has six sisters and one brother. She has worked as a prostitute and a thief. When we spoke, she was on parole for conduct regardless of life. She had stabbed her "man," the father of her second child, after he beat her with a hammer. She says of her childhood:

Well, the only thing I recall is a fight.

How old were you then?

Twelve. I recall I fell down the stairs and got hung up on a nail. My toenail came off. And I remember at the time the pain and it bled. Later on, my mother asked me how I would feel if she went to jail. And I didn't know right from wrong at the time, anyway, you know; I figured they was trying to help her and it's just that I made matters worse because she had stabbed my stepfather so many different ways. She used to beat on him a lot, you know, and she's stronger than him. And I think, at the time he did have a little thing on the side, I don't know, prostitution or whatever you want to call it; but it was something they didn't want me to know. And, they [the police] asked me about what happened and I didn't know how to explain. But I showed them the knife. It was a long knife. And, you know, she got six months in jail. And my stepfather had already gone to the can 'cause he had raped my sister. He raped my sister and she had a baby and she wasn't no more than sixteen. And the baby only lived to two or three years old. The doctor told them, you know . . . and I couldn't do nothin'. My foot was cut, anyway, you know. An' they would always keep me in my pen, you know, so I couldn't get down and put a lotta pressure on my foot. I can remember that. I didn't start gettin' in trouble until I turned twelve, after my sister passed away. She died when she was seventeen. They forgot to take the afterbirth out of her. And that's when I started getting in trouble. I was so close to her. And, after her death, my mother started mistreating me so bad, you know. I would go to church and he [her stepfather] would bring me home 'cause he lived around the block. I'd get home, she nearly took my eye out 'cause my stepfather . . . and I'm still wondering at the time why she's doin' all this fuss over my stepfather. And I started running away. And then the first time I ran, I came back the next day, and I got the worst beatin' I ever got, you know. But I got fed up with she makin' me a slave, you know, stayin' home and babysit, you know, take my money . . . I was workin', baby-sittin'. And made me clean, cook, and all the rest of 'em coulda did it. I ranned . . . and they sent me to Oregon. But the whole time I ran, I met people like I never met before. And I would like, con them outta money, just to get where I wanted to go. And I would turn around and fight 'em because they expected somethin' from me. And I couldn't go back home 'cause I was afraid. And I was runnin' from the law. I got hitched up with some drug man and he was a pimp.

How old were you then?

I was fourteen or fifteen.

Vernetta later returned to her family. It hardly seems possible, but the situation there had deteriorated even further. The rest of her life, from fifteen to twenty-two, is one of running away and getting involved with pimps and pushers and returning home, usually after a run-in with the law. It was difficult to tell just what Vernetta's mental state was then or at the time of the interview. As her own words reveal, she is confused. She may also be mildly retarded. Neither her mental state nor the details of her life were unique among the women in this group.

It is obvious that whether the female runaway is a pushout or not, the unmet emotional needs that precipitated her running away, combined with her very real physical and economic needs once she has run, leave her in a vulnerable position when she hits the streets. She is ripe for a potentially exploitative relationship with a (usually older) "man" or a bottom woman acting in his stead. They may approach her in a tavern, on the street, or in a bus terminal or train station with a sympathetic ear and an offer of food and a place to stay, not to mention the excitement of the nice clothes, money, sex, partying, drinking, and drugs that characterize the more attractive side of the fast life.

If homes offer only a much less glamorous form of exploitation, then these approaches may seem all the more tempting. In contrast to women who come from families with more to offer, where the parents or guardians are relieved (even if confused and angry, as well) at the return of their charges, these families/households may regard their return as an intrusion. The young woman may reluctantly return home to see her child or children occasionally or when she is particularly down and out and without a "man," but sooner or later those ties that pull her to stay will be overcome by the same pressures that forced her to leave initially. Assuming she returns to the streets and does not use this return home as a way of withdrawing from street life permanently, one can usually conclude that the situation at home makes the streets appear, at least temporarily and sporadically, more attractive or that she feels she has no other choice.

Georgia's initial departure from home was precipitated by the sexually aggressive behavior of her stepfather. She says:

> I come from a strange family. I mean me and my mother, we never had any, I guess, mother and daughter love. I had a stepfather. He was real mean and cruel to me. As I grew up, I grew to hate him and he grew to hate me. And when I told my mother things about him, she never did believe me. So, then I started hating her, too. I hated all of 'em. And I told my stepfather's niece that I was going to murder him one day. And she went back and told him. So, he confronted me with it, and I told him: "If I wanted to kill you, I would have caught you while you were sleeping." But he told my mother if I didn't go, he would have to go. She was going to put me in a foster home, but my grandmother took me in. That's when I started running away. My grandmother and me would split cans a pork and beans and they's over there eating steaks. And I'm runnin' around with no shoes when, like my brother and them, they have new sneakers and new short sets and things . . . later, when I was grown and my mother was sick . . . I had been staying off and on with my mother's people . . . and I'd go home, my stepfather would say: "Why don't you get over by your aunt's and your

grandmother's?" And my mother would do whatever my stepfather would say.

Another respondent, Carol, says of her attempt to return home:

> My mother wanted me to come back home then. She says that nothin' I do shocks her; she's beyond shock. So, I went, but it was my father. You see my two kids are mixed. Their fathers are black. My father had a fit. He said the landlord would kick them out. And by this time I had one brother busted for marijuana. And my other brother got busted for carrying my younger brother across the state line which they got him for kidnappin' . . . car theft. I left. My kids went in a foster home.

Runaways Who Are Domestic Network Members

It is not at all unusual for domestic networks and even individual households embedded in domestic networks to contain several circles of kin, pseudo-kin, and friends with varying levels of involvement in street life. In such situations, parents and/or guardians who are aware that their charges may be recruited to street life often react in a manner that is similar to that of parents with greater economic resources. They tend to curtail the activities of these young women to the point where their efforts are seen as unreasonable when young women compare themselves to their peers.

Perhaps because they have a greater awareness of the possibility of recruitment to street life than wealthier parents, these parents and/or guardians seem the most likely to take extreme measures to deal with any early signs of interest in street activity. The first attempts at control often take the form of rigidly enforced curfews and dress codes. Another tactic is to try to make the girl see that her behavior is not in accord with her religious beliefs. Thus, young women recall mothers and/or other female guardians buying them dowdy dresses and insisting that they attend church services daily. One woman describes presenting herself to her mother shortly before they were due to leave for church in such a state of dishevelment that she knew the woman would be too embarrassed to be seen with her at services and would allow her to remain at home.

When such social control tactics failed, these parents and guardians requested the intervention of the juvenile justice system or insisted that the young woman leave home. The former strategy led to situations not unlike those confronted by Marilyn and Jeanne. When these women ran from detention, however, they had domestic network members already plugged into deviant street networks. In these cases they often moved directly in with domestic network members who were making a living by a hustle. In other cases these kin or pseudo-kin made arrangements for them to live with street network members who were not domestic network members. Akeena's recruitment to street hustling illustrates this pattern.

Akeena was imprisoned in the Milwaukee House of Correction. She was an articulate and attractive black woman of eighteen. She had a seventh-grade education and was the youngest of thirteen children. To her knowledge, two of her three sisters had been arrested at least once, as had almost all of her nine brothers. Akeena had no children of her own. At the time of the interview, one brother was in the state maximum security prison and one had just been released. Another brother was in prison in California. Akeena also had a brother who was mentally retarded and had been institutionalized at age twenty-four after having lived at home for most of his childhood. Her father had had a disabling stroke shortly after her birth and lived at home, where he was cared for by his wife. Before that time, Akeena says, she'd been told that he did a "little bit of everything" to earn a living. She knew that he used to make and sell whiskey. Her mother was a day-care worker until her husband's illness, when she stopped working outside the home.

The older women in Akeena's domestic network were Jehovah's Witnesses, and Akeena's mother tried to get her to associate only with others in the church herself. Akeena recalled that, although she first knew about marijuana because her brothers who were still living at home smoked it, she first got high herself in the company of the children of these Jehovah's Witnesses. By the time she was ten, Akeena had been smoking marijuana regularly for over a year and was beginning to get in trouble for truancy. Although she admits that her mother had her hands full, Akeena says of this time:

Me, I always thought, too, that, you know, she used to put the load off on me and all. I always thought that she was always pickin' on me, saying I shouldn't do this, I shouldn't do that. I saw my brothers doin' stuff, you know . . . they stayed out late, they do what they want to do; they have girlfriends coming in the house. Afterwards, she say he better than me; that's how she thinkin'. Sometimes she say, you know: "Harold [her brother], you know, he did this; he got a day's pay, you know. Why can't you be like that?" I'd say: "I'm not him; I'm me." She don't like that, you know, and I don't like her telling me I should do this and I should do the other thing.

When Akeena was eleven, she got picked up by the police with a bunch of other children who had decided to go to a neighboring school and pick a fight with a group of children there. Her mother picked her up at the police station and told her that she either would have to live by her rules, as a good Jehovah's Witness, or find somewhere else to live.

Akeena went to live with three young women who were her older cousins, although she referred to them as "stepsisters." She said:

They was whores. I was stayin' there and they kept tellin' me, you know: "You should try it, you know; the money's good!" I said: "Oh, no. I ain't gonna fuck around." I tried to get a job, you know, eleven years old, talkin' crazy about workin'. Then one of 'em had this date [trick]; he gave her two hundred and fifty dollars. She told me if I just went in the room and rubbed his dick, he'd give me money, too. I went in there: "Give me money first." He gave me a hundred dollars. I came out and another sister went in. He had about a thousand dollars, and we got all of it. From then on, I just acted cool. I said: "Let's go on out; the money's good. I was workin' by myself; I wasn't payin' nobody.

It wasn't long before Akeena was paying someone, however, and had four wives-in-law and a drug habit. At the time of the interview, she had had arrests as a juvenile for prostitution, shoplifting, possession of marijuana, and armed robbery. Six months after her eighteenth birthday, she had seven arrests for prostitution.

If Akeena's mother had not had a string of bad experiences with her other children and had had life a bit easier generally, she might not have been so quick to ask Akeena to leave home or she might have attempted to have her detained as "incorrigible." Akeena would probably have left on bad terms with her mother at some point in any event. Given that the mothers of young women like Akeena are often saddled with their grandchildren when these women start to hustle on a regular basis and can incur other substantial costs associated with their daughters' hustling, Akeena's mother, contemplating these possibilities, may have decided to make it clear to Akeena that she would have to sever all contact if that was the life she wanted to lead. Even when Akeena called on her mother for aid when she was in jail or ill, her mother refused to come to visit her if her "man" was still in the picture. For Akeena's mother there was clearly no middle ground.

The crucial point here is that even when relationships with primary socializers are *completely* undermined, young women like Akeena have ready-made ways of plugging into other parts of their domestic networks that overlap with deviant street networks. It is this fact that makes this category of runaways an empirically and analytically distinct one.

Drug Use

Although many of the women I spoke with had serious drug and alcohol problems, very few describe substance abuse as the thing that caused them to become involved in deviant street networks. Soft drug use may be a contributing factor because it establishes certain behavior patterns and attitudes that make experimentation with drugs, such as heroin, seem less deviant. When experimentation develops into dependence, it increases the woman's attachment to the street life and decreases the possibilities that she will leave it. Drug use probably also increases the likelihood that these women will come in contact with people who lead street lives. For some of them, such people already are part of their lives, however, in the persons of users, if not dealers, who are members of their own households, domestic networks, or neighborhood households. Many young women talked about smoking marijuana or taking speed with siblings, step-siblings, young uncles, aunts, cousins, or friends, but none spoke of being introduced to heavy drugs, such as heroin, in this way. On the contrary, several mentioned having been discouraged by slightly older household members (some of whom were users) from ever getting involved with hard drugs.

The overwhelming majority of women with serious substance abuse problems developed them *after* they were already immersed in the fast life. This should not be surprising given the very young age at which most of these women started breaking ties with home and becoming involved with "men." A repeated observation found in the literature on substance abuse among women is that males are the carriers of illegal drug-use patterns to females. This is principally because the control of the illegal distribution of drugs, especially heroin, is in the hands of men (Bowker 1978b: 65). Even in households where women were recruited by their own brothers to participate in selling marijuana or pills, forging checks, or prostitution, they were not introduced to hard drugs in this way. Rather, there is evidence of rather strong norms against such introductions. These norms are strengthened by the fact that recruitment of this sort is not income-producing and may, in fact, be a further drain on household and personal resources.

The few women for whom substance abuse was the route to involvement in deviant street networks (three of the Hispanic women interviewed might be placed in this category as well as four whites and three blacks) were never completely integrated into these networks. The social world of deviant street activity and the social world of the addict are to a certain extent distinct and incompatible. The chaos that can pervade the lives of addicts, at least episodically, precludes their ever being more than peripheral members of deviant street networks. Powerful structural conditions ensure that many features of the addict's lifestyle make such a woman a less than desirable candidate for cooperative hustling activity.

Women for whom substance abuse was the route to involvement in deviant street networks were at first only marginally part of these networks. They and/or their boyfriends were dealing to members of networks or buying from members. Young women not otherwise involved in street life who had recently been introduced to the use of narcotics (usually by their boyfriends) tended to experience their first real involvement in hustling when they or the men they were with could not, for one reason or another, supply the amount of drugs or kinds of drugs necessary to keep them from getting "a Jones" (withdrawal symptoms). If the men they were with were dealers, it was possible for this situation to be quite a long time in coming. If, for some reason, these men left them, overdosed, or were arrested, it was possible for such women to become major dealers themselves. More often, this was the occasion for the young woman to hit the streets to raise cash. It is important to note that very often this hustling was done on an individual basis and not as a member of a deviant street network, however. The participation of such women in street life, then, may be rather sporadic depending on the stability of their drug source. Intermittent users who are small-time dealers are more likely to actually become active members of deviant street networks as opposed to sporadic lone hustlers than are women who are heavy users and dealers. In other words, although there is a good deal of interaction between women (and the men they associate with) who are heavy users and dealers and the membership of deviant street networks because the former are a source of hard drugs for this membership, the world of the "junkie" (a person addicted to drugs) is really socially and attitudinally a distinct one.

Moreover, offenses such as possession of heroin are punished more severely than most other street crimes. Very often, when addicts are arrested, they are forced to participate while in prison or on probation or parole in drug rehabilitation programs. Even if a woman is living in the community, such programs (as well as lengthy sentences) can place severe restrictions on her freedom of movement. Overall, then, even a "man" who is a heavy drug user himself will prefer to recruit women who are only occasional users.

Not only is it difficult for seriously addicted women to become members of deviant street networks, but, for women who are members, serious addiction may be the first step on the road out of such networks. In fact, several of the women I met were attempting to walk the stroll as "outlaw women" (women without a "man") because no "man" would take a chance on them.

They were either too "hot" (were under the scrutiny of the narcotics squad as well as the vice squad), too "used up" (had become
unattractive because of the lifestyle that accompanies addiction),
or too "strung out" (crazy, desperate, unreliable). For the woman's part, she in turn cannot afford to share her profits with a
"man." In addition, she derives fewer benefits from street life and
is exposed to more dangers than other women because she is not
part of a deviant street network.

The only time she may be allowed to participate in the usual
round of exchanges of information and social and emotional
support that is the focus of deviant street network membership is
before she is used up and when she's clean (probably because she's
been in jail). During clean periods, she may prefer, if she has the
education and social support, to try to get a straight job.

In short, when the addict most needs the deviant street network, she has the least to give it and is, in fact, perceived as a
threat to it. Thus, she is spurned, exploited, or accepted only
warily by its membership. On the other hand, when she needs it
least, it is there for her. In addition, whereas most street women
are "in the life" for economic reasons, because it affords them a
certain (albeit ephemeral) independence, for the excitement, or
because of the persuasiveness of a "man," addicts are in it not as a
career in and of itself but as a means to an end, a score. In a very
real sense, such a woman may not have the requisite career commitment. She may even feel, as one woman did, that that sort of
activity is beneath her even though she has stooped to it when her
need for drugs was very great.

One case illustrates the entry and contact pattern very well.
Kathy is a twenty-six-year-old white woman who has had three
children. She put her youngest child up for adoption, and her
first child lives with her ex-husband. She has two younger sisters
and an older brother. None of them has had a run-in with the law
although two of them are very occasional drug users. At the time
of the interview she was awaiting transfer from the House of
Correction to Taycheedah. She had been convicted of multiple
forgeries.

Kathy seems to have gotten involved in problematic drug
use following a particularly traumatic domestic crisis. She did not
have a juvenile record, was never truant, and never ran away. She
started using marijuana and barbiturates shortly after her parents

divorced. She was twelve years old at the time. Her father was a truck driver with a serious drinking problem. Her mother was a housewife. After the divorce, her mother was on welfare for several years, but has worked outside the home since that time.

Kathy remembers her parents' having terrible fights when she was a child during which her father would beat her mother. She recalls being exceptionally upset about their divorce. She blamed her mother for divorcing her father—with whom she had been very close—and fought bitterly with her about this. After two years of smoking marijuana and taking downers, Kathy started shooting heroin with her boyfriend, who had also been providing her with the other drugs. Soon she was also dealing. This continued until she was a senior in high school. She describes this time in the following way:

> I went to Catholic school. I made it to the twelfth grade. About two months before I graduated, I got hepatitis from shooting dope. I ended up in the hospital. That's when my mother first found out I was shooting dope. The doctor told her that was the only possible way I could have got it because it was serum hepatitis. . . . Well, okay, I met my husband about nine months after I got this hepatitis and went with him for a while and then I busted up with him. And, uh, I wasn't shooting dope anymore. I had stopped. I just turned nineteen and I started shooting again. We got married and everything was going real well for us. But the dope got into the act, got into our lives. And soon after that happened we ended up splitting up. It was just that there was nothing left for us. I mean sexual desires weren't being met. We didn't care about each other as much as we did the dope. The dope always came first.

Kathy's ex-husband has since stopped dealing and using. He's told Kathy that he doesn't want anything to do with her as long as she uses heroin. She wasn't able to deal and use without him, however. Her habit was costing her two to three hundred dollars a day. Although she was never caught, she earned money as a prostitute and by forging checks and dealing. During that time, she was marginally involved in deviant street networks, mainly ones with significant drug dealing and use among their shifting membership. Her most recent child was fathered by a man who was, at the time we spoke, in a state correctional facility for armed robbery. She claims that he doesn't "do drugs," and that, in fact, he didn't commit the armed robbery. Information from other sources, however, leads me to believe that he is deeply involved in deviant street networks in Milwaukee. If Kathy does link up with him when they are both free again, the chances of her becoming involved in deviant street networks herself are quite high, while the chances of her staying clean are very slight. While they are in prison, both of these people will have expanded their circle of acquaintances who have at one time been members of deviant street networks.

As mentioned above, those, like Kathy, for whom substance abuse was the route to at least sporadic involvement in deviant street networks tended to be white or Hispanic rather than black.[2] The total number of Hispanic women I spoke with was only four. My research findings, however, are congruent with those of Joan Moore (1982). The heavy involvement of Hispanic street women in narcotics is beyond dispute. Moore finds narcotics dealing and use to be an intimate part of barrio culture in East Los Angeles, her research site. A similar situation seems to exist in Milwaukee.[3]

Women are introduced to narcotics use by boyfriends, but also by girlfriends. Whereas it seems to take a family crisis or some other major disruption in household organization to propel both white and Hispanic women into heavy use, Hispanic women seem more likely to be introduced to hard drug use within their own extended households. The difference between Hispanic women and white women seems to be a matter of availability and the strength of competing norms governing use. Not only are the norms against use, especially among peers, weaker for Hispanic women, but the values that foster use are deeply embedded in the culture with which the young woman is likely to be surrounded.

2. A recent study of female offenders undertaken by the U.S. General Accounting Office contains the following relevant statement: "For white and Indian offenders, drug violations seem to be one of the two most common crimes [the other being forgery/fraud]; for Hispanic women, it is by far their major crime. Most violators are users, not pushers or organizers" (1979: 17).

3. See also Alberto G. Mata's Ph.D. dissertation, "The Drug Street Scene: An Ethnographic Study of Mexican Youth in South Chicago" (1978), for similar data for that city.

In addition, the fact that Mexico is a major source of heroin in Milwaukee as well as in Los Angeles means that there is automatic availability of the drug in the community in which the young woman resides. The pattern of intermittent lone hustling for the already seriously addicted woman and the deeper involvement in deviant street networks of the occasional user/small-time dealer seems to parallel the pattern found among white women. If the relatively small proportion of black women in this category is not simply a function of sampling technique, and I suspect it is not, it may be attributed to the fact that they tend to be recruited to street life earlier than either whites or Hispanics via other routes—that is, before drug use becomes problematic.

Incest as a Factor in Running Away and Drug Use

My initial interviews did not contain any questions on incest or sexual abuse generally, but several young women described incest as something that led to their running away or their use of drugs. In subsequent interviews, then, when women described household situations in which they had been physically abused by men or situations in which the main source of familial conflict was between a young woman and her father, stepfather, or other male authority figure, and it seemed appropriate to ask the questions, I did.[4] By this very unsystematic method, I found two cases of incest among the white women (8%) and eight among the black women (20%). All but one of these instances of incest seemed to have precipitated running away or problematic drug use and promoted recruitment to the fast life. The exception was one black woman who had a sexual relationship with her father; she had not known him as a child but had tracked him down after she had already been hustling for a number of years. At the time, the woman was running from the police and her father lived out of state and offered her refuge. This was the only instance where the sexual involvement seemed to have been entered into voluntarily.

4. I did not make this an area that I routinely asked questions about, however, because there were many life histories to which it was clearly not relevant. Moreover, where it was not, introducing such a sensitive topic might have had a negative effect on the quality of the interview.

Although my data on this topic are neither systematic enough nor extensive enough to draw any conclusions from, my hunch is that this is a much more important factor in patterns of running away and drug use and, thus, in recruitment to deviant street networks than is generally acknowledged. It is also my belief that the experience of emotional distancing during sexual contact that incest victims often describe is too like the psychological state described by prostitutes when they are servicing a trick for one not to be a sort of rehearsal for the other. In those cases, sexual exploitation on the street seems but an extension of sexual exploitation in the family.

The important point to be made here is that incest is probably a contributing factor in the recruitment of young women to deviant street networks. In addition, it is a factor that needs to be taken seriously and examined more closely.

Although a possible link between incest and running away has been noted before in the literature, it has usually been interpreted as an unconscious psychological construct, a manifestation of the girl's "unresolved oedipal feelings," or some such.[5] In other words, the reality of the incestuous activity has been challenged. My data lead me to believe that in many cases the fear of incest is more than simply an unconscious one. As a matter of fact, two of the male relatives described by Milwaukee informants as sexually abusive were convicted of having incestuous relationships with more than one young woman in their households. Nor is such behavior found exclusively within the disorganized households of pushouts.

The Three Recruitment Routes

Young women in Milwaukee are recruited to deviant street networks in three different ways: through domestic networks, by running away, and as a result of drug use. The route via the domestic network is most often taken by poor black women,

---

5. For example, a study entitled "The Runaway Girl" by Ames Robey contains the following: "In a large proportion of cases, there is considerable indication that the girl runs away from home to ward off the unconscious threat of an incestuous relationship with her father, the fear of the resultant dissolution of the family, and the concurrent depression" (1969: 127).

while the route via drug use appears to be taken most often by poor Hispanic women. The route via running away, however, seems to be available to young women with little regard for race, ethnicity, or social class.

The separate consideration of each route is not meant to suggest that in every case one can say without hesitation which particular path was followed. At times there is a certain blurring of the structural conditions that seem to indicate one pattern with conditions that indicate another pattern and the actual recruitment involves so many deviant activities' all being engaged in seemingly simultaneously that it is difficult to say just what the recruitment route was. Theoretically, a young woman may have a highly crimogenic domestic network, be a habitual runaway, and be well on the road to becoming an addict all at the same time. Although this mixed pattern was observed, a causally dominant route was usually discernable. The point is that there may be more overlap in the behaviors actually exhibited and the structural conditions that appear to have promoted them than the separate treatments offered here suggest.

The phenomena described here that seem to be of especial importance are a set of structural conditions that account for a certain race effect. It is clear, for example, that black females participate in deviant street activity in Milwaukee to a degree that far surpasses the proportion of the city's population they constitute. Although it is impossible to estimate what proportion of women on the hustle in the city are black, my guess would be that it is well over half. The overrepresentation of black women is especially striking when one considers that, of the people living in the Milwaukee SMSA in 1976, only 8.2 percent were black (Edari 1978: 86). If active involvement in prostitution is an indicator of participation in deviant street activity generally, this observation is consistent with Cohen's ecological study of street prostitution in New York City in which he estimates that about 45.3 percent of prostitutes there are black (1980: 65).

Given the number of poor white women who could wind up on the street and the number of poor black women with that same potential, far more black women than white women seem to actually make the trip. It has been argued in this chapter and the last that one possible reason for this is that black women have a greater number of avenues open to them that lead to the street than do white women, with Hispanic women located somewhere in between. Black women have access to all the routes available to other women with the addition of what seems to be a rather well-traveled route, the route directly via the domestic network. Hispanic women, it would appear, have available to them the route open to white women and also are more likely than whites to have the routes via drug use and extended household available to them. For this reason, white women seem to be afforded a certain degree of protection from being recruited via some of these routes that is afforded neither black nor Hispanic women.

There is another interesting way of making the same observation. It is the *organization* of households among poor blacks into domestic networks that promotes the recruitment of young black women directly to deviant street networks. It is often a situation of household *disorganization,* at least as it is indicated by intense conflict between young women and their caretakers, that is most likely to promote the recruitment of white and Hispanic women to deviant street networks, however, via running away and drug use. The impetus that the women who take these routes derive from familial conflict affects young black women as well. Their actual recruitment, then, resembles that of white and Hispanic women to the degree that they are not members of familial networks that extend to the streets. To the degree that they are, these networks may play an indirect role in their recruitment. At the very least, they may provide a refuge for young black women who sever their ties to their immediate caretakers. More often they also are the context within which initiation into the fast life occurs. Whether the intersection of domestic and deviant street networks provides direct or indirect access to the street, however, they do afford young black women greater opportunities for being recruited to deviant street networks than are available to either white or Hispanic women.

CHAPTER
V

Living the Fast Life: The Unique Conditions of Hustling as Women's Work

Once she has been recruited to street life, there are several groups of factors that influence the direction of a young woman's hustling career. The first group includes her contacts with the criminal justice system, her fertility and general health, the effect of street life and age on her physical attractiveness, her drug and alcohol use, and the hustling activities of the "men" with whom she is involved. Another set of factors includes her relationship to her family/household of origin after recruitment and usually, not unrelatedly, the changing arrangements for the care of any children she had before being recruited to the streets and any born while hustling. Over time, many of these factors are, in turn, modified by the dynamics of the woman's hustling itself. Thus, physical attractiveness, drug and alcohol use, relationship to family/household of origin, nature and frequency of contacts with the criminal justice system, and fertility and general health are all often influenced by the activities, relationships, events, behavior patterns, and psychological states peculiar to female street hustlers.

Relationships with Family/Household of Origin

Pushouts and women whose departure from home has been preceded by heated conflict with parents and/or guardians are much less likely to sustain contact with primary caretakers from their families/households of origin than women who have been recruited directly through the interface of familial networks and deviant street networks. Even when primary caretakers have been violently opposed to hustling as a career for their female charges and when the knowledge of initial hustling activity has been verbally condemned or physically punished, the kin of women recruited directly via familial networks are likely to find some way of accommodating the young woman's new identity and the new behavior that accompanies it. An uneasy accommodation is also the response of primary caretakers of women whose recruitment has occurred as a result of running away or drug use but who have been indirectly recruited through the interface of familial networks and deviant street networks. The degree of periodic conflict surrounding the street activities of these women is greater, however, than when women have been recruited directly via familial networks. Of course, many of the latter parents and/or guardians have gone to great lengths to try to prevent recruitment. In fact, it has often been the fear of just such an occurrence that was the impetus for the conflicts that preceded the young woman's running away or problematic drug use in the first place. The fact that a well-known proscription has been violated is not easily forgotten.

No matter which route to the street they have taken, women who have had children before being recruited are more likely to sustain contact with their families/households of origin than those who have not. In every instance, women from familial networks who have begun to hustle regularly and have children either arrange for a familial network member to care for the children or are forced by the members of their households as well as by the realities of their new lives to make such arrangements. In most cases, such an arrangement is simply taken for granted. The caretaker is most often whoever had taken care of the woman herself, usually her mother or grandmother or, less frequently, another female relative or the mother or grandmother of the child's father. There seems to be general agreement that such an arrangement is in the best interest of the children. The young woman is then expected to contribute to the support of the household in which her children reside, although it is usually anticipated that her contributions will be irregular both in terms of their frequency and their amounts.

Young women who have not grown up in domestic networks are much more likely to have given any children born before their involvement in street life up for adoption. Some of these children have been placed in foster homes at some point of their mothers' contact with the criminal justice system. There are several instances here as well, however, where the children are cared for by the father's family or the young woman's mother. These women are also much more likely to have married the fathers of their children than are women from domestic networks. If the marriage has been dissolved and the father or his family has taken responsibility for the children, this is likely to have been done with some degree of acrimony and as the result of a court battle. Such formal proceedings are rare among women from domestic networks. In effect, this sort of arrangement often means that the young woman has no access or only limited access to her children. It also means that she has no claim to AFDC payments.

There is a clear racial/ethnic difference here. Whites simply seem not to have developed the pattern of child-keeping characteristic of poor minority members. Even where the mother of a white woman takes care of her daughter's children, the gesture is much more likely to be seen as an act of generosity than as an unquestioned matter of duty. Generally speaking, however, in these cases, as in the cases of women whose families/households are embedded in domestic networks, women who have had children prior to becoming involved in hustling and who still have custody of those children are much more likely than those who do not to sustain contact with their families/households of origin albeit contact often filled with tension.

Continued contact with domestic networks that interface with street networks provide a greater exposure to involvement in a variety of scams for some women. These are contacts with deviant street networks that may or may not overlap with the contacts with street networks the young woman no doubt already has. Supportive relationships with members of her family/- household of origin may also have the countervailing effect of providing the young woman a refuge when, for one reason or another, she wants or needs temporarily to leave street life.

Because of the very good chance that the caretakers who are offering the young women emotional support are also caring for their children, these elder women are in a unique position to influence the hustling behavior of young female street hustlers.

They have several options open to them that they can use as threats. They can seek custody of the children themselves, thus becoming the legitimate recipient of AFDC benefits for the children should they be deemed eligible. The psychological effect of the loss of custody on the young mother should also not be minimized. In addition, because they are in close contact with these women, often even when they are on the run, these caretakers are in a position to inform the authorities of their whereabouts and activities should they decide it is in their interest, the interest of the children they are keeping, or the interest of the young women for them to do so. These sorts of options seem to be acted upon or at least threatened to "slow down" (place limitations upon) a woman who is perceived to be "moving too fast" (so involved in street life that health and welfare are in immediate danger) in order to get her to make financial contributions to the support of the household, spend more time with her children, and/or curb her drug use. Caretakers may also attempt to control their former female charges when they think they are in physical danger. Georgia describes her mother's efforts to curtail her drug use and hustling as follows:

> At first I thought I was going into a nervous breakdown. And my mother, she got to talking about puttin' me out and gettin' me locked up. She said: "You get yourself together or we're going to have to put you away." And I went down to a hundred and five pounds. I was really fading away, you know. And my mother said: "What about your kids? Don't you think they need a mother, too? Think about it." And my mother walked out the door and just left me, you know, in suspense like. What should I do?

Ultimately, the older woman can threaten to refuse to care for the children. Action on such a threat could immeasurably complicate the life of the young woman but, in fact, seems rarely to be taken unless the caretaker herself becomes unable to care for the child due to ill health, old age, or other problems. Particularly for a woman who has developed a drug dependency, pressure of this sort may have the unintended consequence of forcing her more deeply into street life in an attempt to provide for her own needs as well as the needs of her household of origin.

Young women who have been "cut loose" (rejected) by their
families/households, either prior to recruitment, at recruitment,
or later because they have become too much of an emotional and
financial drain, become completely dependent on their own
resourcefulness. Those who do not have children or have lost
custody of their children have no claim on the welfare system
through AFDC although they may still be able to qualify temporarily for the less desirable benefits available through General
Assistance. In fact, this usually means that they become completely vulnerable to the "men" who control the streets and/or to
their drug habits. If they have been forced to assume responsibility for their children, the physical and emotional abuse of these
children is not unlikely even if they are placed in daycare or with
a hired sitter for a good part of the day or evening. Children who
remain in their mother's care while she continues to hustle risk
becoming part of the next generation of pushouts. Another not
uncommon occurrence is for these children to be placed in foster
homes when their mothers are convicted of felonies and sent to
Taycheedah for lengthy stays or come to the attention of social
service agencies and are deemed unfit. Only women who are able
to set up scams where they are relatively safe from arrest and have
some control over the conditions of their work have lives stable
enough to care adequately for children themselves. Georgia describes trying to juggle childcare and the hassles of dealing with
fellow deviant street network members:

> I had got accused . . . once you're known for getting money
> and you're around and somethin' come up missing, you're
> gonna get accused. And it was like four other women was in
> the house and my "man" and his brother. They said I took
> five hundred and fifty dollars that was under the mattress.
> So, I left the house that day. I was staying back by my
> grandmother. But that potty chair and things was still mine,
> so I felt that it was still a parta my house too, and my kids.
> So we goes over there and we spent the night that night. But
> I forgot to bring my little girl's clothes for school. So I left
> and got the clothes and came back. I took her to school and
> around lunchtime I brought her back. That's when my
> "man" and his brother . . . closed me off in the bedroom
> and started to beat me. I was flying around the room like

somebody would take a ball and bounce it up against the wall. And I didn't know what was happenin' to the kids.

The only hustling activity that street women engage in that seems to be compatible with caring for small children is fairly high-level drug dealing. As the women say, however: "The 'man' holds the bag." It is not easy for women to achieve such positions in the drug trade, nor are they likely to occupy them for very long.

Children

Generally speaking, female street hustlers do not involve their children in their work. In certain circumstances, most particularly in shoplifting and drug traffic, women describe using children as "fronts." Drugs are secreted in baby clothes or diaper bags, and strollers are used as caches for boosted items. Usually if children stay with their mothers or are in her care at all, however, it is only intermittently. The tempo of hustling, the type of scam, the pattern of arrests and confinements, the extent of guilt feelings surrounding the issue of mothering, and the willingness of kin to take responsibility for children all influence whether or not youngsters stay with their mothers and for how long.

The inability or unwillingness of these women to care for their own children on a regular basis and their resultant feelings of inadequacy as mothers leave them open to manipulation not only by the members of their own families/households but also by the "men" who manage their hustling. It is common for a "man" who wants a woman to work for him to buy presents for her children, to support them, and to participate to some extent in their care. Such arrangements are usually short-lived. The dynamics of hustling as well as the geographic mobility characteristic of those attempting to elude the authorities are certain to undermine these attempts at domesticity. Jealousies and other conflicts also develop when males who have fathered one or more of the children and who are sometimes also hustlers seek to visit their children or object to these arrangements. When a woman has left a "man" who has not posted bail for her or who has beaten her, the man often uses the one surefire technique for renewing contact with her when such efforts would otherwise be rebuked: he pretends to have information about a sick or injured child. Vice officers are also reportedly not above using such ploys to gain access to women.

Several women interviewed described situations in which they were on the run in the state or had run to another state to escape prosecution and returned home to see children on their birthdays or other special occasions or when they heard they were ill. This sort of behavior sometimes led to their arrest. Loretta, a black woman with more arrests for serious crimes than was usual for these women, describes one such instance:

> I was fightin' with a woman my "man" was goin' with that I didn't know. I pulled my knife outta the pouch in my bra. I remember cutting her. . . . And I just panicked. And I's scared. So we run. I would write my people and send them twenty-five dollars in the mail. I would go way out somewhere and stick the letter and the money order in the mailbox so they wouldn't know where I'd be. We found out that my son had sickle-cell trait, that he had blood in his urine, a kidney infection. And at this time my son turned three. I went home, but that was a stupid idea because the police were watchin' my daddy's house to see if I would come there to see my son. That's how I finally got picked up.

Lastly, there were women who said that the needs of their children motivated them to hustle when they would have preferred straight work, when they knew the risk of apprehension or street violence was high, or when to do so meant leaving the children alone or with someone they didn't trust.

Children, then, are often used to manipulate female street hustlers.[1] They are also sometimes a force motivating behavior that leads to risk-taking and arrest. Alternatively, children and/or children's caretakers may also be the cause of both temporary retreats from street life and less active participation in it. The women interviewed who had for the most part withdrawn from street life said that the knowledge that their children were grow-

---

1. Probation and parole officers also use the children of female offenders as leverage in shaping their behavior. In addition, state legislatures have recently made attempts to write laws that have a similar effect. In California, for example, a woman who uses heroin during her pregnancy may be charged with child abuse at the birth of her child.

ing to adulthood without knowing them very well or that they failed to understand the nature of their mothers' lives was a factor in their withdrawal. Active female street hustlers were also dismayed over such situations. They often spoke with feeling about the fact that their children called another woman "momma." Given the dynamics of hustling and the lack of legitimate options available to them, however, it is unlikely that concern for children alone would motivate a permanent withdrawal from hustling for many of the women interviewed. This is most likely the case because of the ambiguous effect of children on a female street hustler's career. On the one hand, children are a moral force militating against involvement in street life, while, on the other, they are responsibilities that promote it and sometimes physical links to "men" involved in it.

Contacts with the Criminal Justice System

Among the women I interviewed, female hustlers who had been working the streets of Milwaukee and other cities for several years were very likely to have accumulated so many arrests that some of them literally had difficulty keeping track of them all. Each arrest for prostitution and shoplifting (the two most frequent misdemeanors committed by fairly recent recruits to street life along with prostitution-related offenses such as disorderly conduct and vagrancy) usually resulted in probation and/or a fine. Very shortly after starting to accumulate arrests, women were also being picked up for the non-payment of those fines and having their probation revoked for various reasons including more criminal activity. As a result, it would not be unusual for a woman simultaneously to be sitting in jail awaiting trial on a new charge, to be responsible for the payment of at least parts of fines, and to be awaiting hearings for the violation of probation constituted by her new criminal activity. These hearings may, in turn, activate stayed or withheld sentences on old charges. If the woman has been "travelin'" at all, she may also have warrants outstanding or cases pending in other parts of the state or, indeed, in other states.

Although some of the female hustlers interviewed had a difficult time keeping track of their arrests, they had a remarkable ability to describe the intricacies of the sanctions imposed as a result of these arrests at any point in time. In terms of their work, it was the penalties that were important, not the arrests. They were the "bottom line," so to speak, for although the costs of street life were many and far-reaching for these women, "fines and time" were some of the more predictable of them. The following descriptions by incarcerated or recently incarcerated women, who for the moment were not committing new crimes, were typical:

JOYCE

The first time I got in trouble I was sixteen, okay? That's when they sent me to Oregon. I met a girl that I became pretty tight with as we knew some of the same people from the outside. She was there for shoplifting. So, after she left, I got in touch with her, and we started shoplifting. The first time I caught a case it was at Gimbels downtown, and they dismissed it. They kept me in jail overnight. I caught several more cases out in the suburbs. I paid a fine, got outta jail, got a few days, paid a fine, and so on. As the years went on I kept getting shoplifting cases. So the first time, I think it was nineteen seventy-six, I had six cases. I had one felony and five misdemeanors. The judge gave me six months, straight six months on that. I got out, and a couple of months later I caught another shoplifting case. Okay, the judge sent me out here [House of Correction] again. He gave me ninety days' work release, got out and got another shoplifting case. I just slid through the county jail 'cause they didn't find out about anything before. See, I went into the file room with my lawyer and took my files. I got fined fifty dollars. It took them a while to get the files back from Madison where another copy is stored. So, when they found out all this back information, I got another case. They put me in the county jail. My PO decided to let me go because she knowed I was going to jail anyway. I ended up catching another felony. The charge was repeated three times, all right? I had to be charged with felony twice. The first time they took me, they dropped the felony and gave me six months, okay? They then sentenced me to one year out here, four years on probation, and a five-year stayed sentence. So, as of July first, I'll be incarcerated eight months altogether.

So, when you get out, you'll be on probation five years? [I was very confused.]

I'll be on probation five years? No, three years after I get out of here because I still have five stayed left. I've had three years of probation.

What happens if you get caught again?

It's TY [Taycheedah], no doubt about it, and I'll have to do twenty-two months on that five years.

ROSEMARY

They gave me two years' probation. Then I had, oh, no, the first time, ah, they didn't give me nothin'. I didn't go. I was scared to go back to court; I walked out. I didn't want to do a lot of time. So, then, I went back to the streets and I caught another case. Then Judge Metz put me on probation for two years. Then I caught another case. They're the one that gave me . . . they dropped it to disorderly conduct, gave me thirty days out here [House of Correction], but they gave me time served, so I only had to do twelve days. And then I got revoked. For two years' probation, they gave me six months. So I have to do four-and-a-half months.

BETSY

What I was doin' in there [House of Correction] was for old loitering and shoplifting and disorderly. And it cost three hundred sixty-six dollars for me to get out. It was a thousand dollars all the way up to last Thursday and it dropped down to three hundred sixty-six dollars. So I had to pay or do until October for three hundred sixty-six dollars.

How come it dropped down?

Because five of them ran consecutive and four of them carried thirty days and one for a disorderly. He gave me two hundred thirty-eight dollars or six months and that was the max on a disorderly so that as, like I say, there was six of them, one ran consecutive, so the consecutive don't start until six months is up and that's only fourteen days for a hundred twenty-eight dollars. So I have three hundred sixty-six dollars, you know? Then I'll still be on probation. By me not having' a "man" when I came in here, I had to wait to use my welfare money to get out.

JEANNE

Why don't you tell me about the first time you caught a case?

Ah, it was two years ago. It was just for a bad check, okay? It was my checking account, but I didn't have the money in the bank. And I was separated from my husband at the time. And I wanted, needed, stuff for the kids, and I figured, well, I'll get the money and pay it before it gets . . . you know. But, they didn't, you know, they got a hold of me, and it was for like two hundred dollars' worth of checks. So, I got, I went in front of Judge Roberts, and he gave me two years' probation. So then during that two years, which I'm still going on, my husband gets into this scam. He receives stolen merchandise from a good friend of his, right? We brought it in the house. I knew it was stolen, but, you know, I didn't say anything 'cause it was a big console TV and three stereos, a microwave oven, all good stuff, so. Turned out a neighbor came over and she said: "What, is that all hot or something?" I said: "Yeah." I was just kidding her. So, what she did is, later on she got angry at my husband, so she went and turned us in at the police department. And they got us for receiving stolen goods. And the guy that he bought it from was a good friend of his. So, then they arrested us again and I was already on probation. My husband had a clean record, and the kid that robbed the house, he had a clean record. So, Judge Emer gave me, um, ten days out here [House of Correction] on Huber time [work release]. But then if I broke my probation from Emer, during this two years, I'd be out here for six months. That's what I'm in here for now. So, then, let's see, then I got picked up for shoplifting. And that time I had a different probation officer and he let me go. He didn't revoke me. So, then, I, um, a month ago, a check came back. They put out another warrant for me. This was a check from a year ago. So, then, for that check I broke my probation again. But I still have to go to court in September for the check, you know, plus I have to go in front of Judge Emer for breaking probation. So I have two cases, you know, to go in front of . . . and in the last coupla months before this, I was going through the cupboards one day and came across these blank checks. What set me out to do it, I don't know, but I wrote a lot of them. They'll find out soon. Then I don't know what.

Surprisingly, legal fees were not usually problematic. Most of these women were automatically deemed indigent for the purposes of determining entitlement to legal assistance because of their status as welfare recipients. As a result they would be assigned a legal aide (public defender) for their defense or to represent them in revocation hearings. Most female street hustlers in Milwaukee pleaded guilty to the charges, whatever they were, and waived their right to a jury trial. To do otherwise would have increased their costs of working. If they could not make bail, there would be the direct cost of jail time before the trial. There would also be the indirect cost of foregone earnings while in jail. The women also believed, probably correctly, that their chances for leniency were better with most judges than they would have been with a jury and that juries would probably find them guilty in any event.

A woman back on the streets with a fine is, then, often working at least part of the time to pay her debt to the state for her last case. If she hired a private attorney who did not insist on the money up front, she may also be working to pay him or her as well. Since many attorneys do demand payment in advance, there is also the possibility that she is repaying whoever loaned her the fees. In short, contacts with the criminal justice system increase her need for fast money by increasing the costs to her of hustling.

One advantage of being involved with a "good" (successful and dependable) "man," or an infatuated trick, and of good relations with one's family/household members is that they may be a source of funds for bail, fines, or jail canteen money when they are needed. A "man" or kinsperson who will pay for a private attorney is viewed as rendering an exceptional service unless the charge is a very serious one. Help with criminal justice costs from family/household members is usually forthcoming only early in a female's hustling career as a matter of course, however. The frequency of such a need causes both good "men" and family/household members to discourage activities, including uncontrolled drug use, that increase street costs. Indeed, one reason for a "woman" to conclude that her "man" is "nothin' but a pimp" is for him to encourage her, or force her with threats of violence, to take unnecessary risks.

The help of kinspersons and lovers seems to be motivated alternately by genuine concern and some calculation of return. Prior demands on resources and the likelihood of future demands are certainly also part of the calculus here. This is true to some degree of both good "men" and of family/household members who derive some benefit from the earnings of street women. The point in a woman's career when such demands are being made as well as her current drug use, then, has an impact on the willingness of significant others to help her, as do their own personal expectations for future gain. Some family/household members will refuse to respond because the woman has been such a drain on family/household resources in the past; others may feel that incarceration will slow down a woman who is moving too fast and thus may refuse to come to her aid for what they see as "her own good." "Men" are more likely to make such judgments on strictly economic grounds. A man whom women would define as a "good" "man," that is, a "man" with a real emotional attachment to his "woman," would, of course, also consider the attachment.

The experience of jail itself is one that is more painful for female street hustlers in Milwaukee than for male hustlers for several reasons. "Men" can call on other "men" for aid, whereas "women" are unlikely to be friendly enough with other "women" who are in a position to help them to ask for their assistance. This situation is at least in part the result of competition among

"women" for "men" and of the fact that "men" deliberately
undermine the networks of "women" so as to control them more
easily. In addition, the female hustlers interviewed usually had
fewer personal financial resources to draw upon than their
"men." This made them dependent on others who, for various
reasons, were often not dependable.

When women are detained, they frequently use their one
phone call to inform whoever is in charge of their children to
make the necessary arrangements. This call usually also serves to
inform their families/households of their need for assistance. If
their kinspersons are willing and have the resources, they may
come to their aid. Very often, however, a woman's call does not do
double duty. If it is her "man" who normally bails her out and
her family/household members will not communicate with him
or cannot get in touch with him, then the woman will sit in jail.
In this case, she is, at least at the time of the study, not entitled to
make a second phone call.[2] Having responsibility for children,
then, can mean that a woman will spend more time in jail before
having her case heard than a similarly situated male.

Another factor that makes confinement especially difficult is
that the facilities in which street women are likely to be held are
basically institutions for men. As compared to time in Taycheedah Correctional Institution *for Women,* incarceration in either
the Milwaukee County Jail or the Milwaukee House of Correction is, for this reason, viewed as "hard time." In both facilities,
because of the relatively small numbers of women, provisions
made for the health, education, religious worship, drug rehabilitation, exercise, and job counseling of men were systematically
denied women or were periodically unavailable. Women also
reported being approached by men employed at these institutions
with proposals for sexual services in exchange for certain
privileges.

The pain of confinement is also increased due to the practice
of routinely running checks on those proposed by the women as

2. This practice has changed as the result of a study by the Benedict Center for
   Criminal Justice in Milwaukee, which stressed the costs to the county of
   enforcing the "one telephone call rule" in cases of women with children.
   The inconvenience and cost of permitting an additional phone call was
   shown to be far outweighed by the savings that would accrue to the county
   as a result of the shortened jail stays of these women.

acceptable visitors or those visitors who just show up at the appropriate time and place. Given that outstanding warrants are likely to be discovered during such checks, many of the people whose physical presence would comfort a confined woman come to visit only at some risk. The women I talked to generally enjoyed seeing their children when confined although some found such visits an embarrassment. Often those who might bring children cannot or will not do so, however. Milwaukee women incarcerated in Taycheedah, for example, are not terribly accessible by public transportation and the ride takes almost two hours. Moreover, the facilities for such visits are dismal. Even the House of Correction is some distance from Milwaukee in rural Franklin. Thus, confinement can be a lonely ordeal.

For women who have been in the state facility for female juvenile delinquents (Oregon) the conditions may not have been especially frightening, but they are to be avoided nonetheless. Since increasing contacts with the criminal justice system are apt to result in increasingly long periods of incarceration, women are likely to look for scams that carry with them less likelihood of arrest as they age and scams that produce faster money. With age and the physical wear of street life, then, the costs of contacts with the criminal justice system increase and the chances of being "rescued" by "men," infatuated tricks, or kinspersons decrease. For this reason, the tendency is for women to look for safer scams. The catch is that scams for which one is less likely to be arrested are also often those that carry heavier penalities.

Although the time spent in jail or the House of Correction is often painful and to be avoided if possible, female street hustlers in Milwaukee generally look upon it as an occupational hazard. Apart from putting a halt to drug use or at least temporarily reducing it, the time spent in either of the two local facilities has little discernible deterrent or rehabilitative effect on the street women intermittently incarcerated there. What it does do is to make female street hustlers reconsider their methods. Exposure to similarly situated women leads to greater sophistication with regard to criminal activity and greater wariness of "men." The need for close personal relationships, however, as well as the need for protection means that this wariness is only rarely translated into completely independent hustling. Although both facilities are sex-segregated, contact between the sexes in those institutions is frequent and the women I talked with often met or learned of males who would become their future "men."

All this means that the search for safer scams is accompanied by the search for really good "men" and/or scams that allow a greater degree of independence and autonomy. For street women these desires often motivate efforts to become bottom women or to achieve a similar status vis-à-vis other female street hustlers so that one is one step removed from the risk of arrest, but still benefits from the scams of those over whom one has authority. A woman may, simultaneously, engage in her own scams and those of her "man." A really good "man" engages in hustling with his bottom woman; it is simply an indication of their mutual trust. These activities are apt to be more serious (and potentially more lucrative) than the prostitution, shoplifting, and petty frauds, forgeries, and drug deals committed by women newly recruited to street life.

Women who are successful at achieving this desired status are eventually arrested on one or more felony charges. If they are convicted, their history of petty criminal activities combines with their most recent offense and usually results in a sentence of several years in Taycheedah. Those of my respondents who had done time in Taycheedah had been affected by the prison experience in a way that women who had cumulatively spent equivalent amounts of time in local jails and the House of Correction had not. If they had not graduated from high school or received their GEDs before this time, they usually received them in Taycheedah. Those qualified and interested also had the opportunity to take college courses while there. Training is also available in cosmetology, data processing, auto mechanics, and general clerical work. Even the female street hustlers interviewed at Metro Center, an institution designed to ease the transition from Taycheedah to free society and one in which only women thought to be good risks are held, however, said that they intended to return to hustling at least as a sideline. They were more reticent than women who had not been in Taycheedah and intended to hustle very selectively or regularly only at very low-risk scams, but it was simply inconceivable to them that they might stop hustling altogether.

Drug Use, Fertility, and General Health

Drug dependency did not seem to motivate participation in street life for many of the women interviewed. This statement needs to be tempered by a reiteration of the observation elaborated upon in Chapter IV, however. There was a clear race/ethnicity effect here. Hispanic and white women were more likely than black women to go on the streets because of a *need* for drugs rather than, or in addition to, increased contacts with deviant network members because of occasional drug use. It is because the majority of street women in Milwaukee were black that the statement above is a generally accurate one. For most women interviewed, drug use became problematic only after they were already on the streets. Even at this point many female street hustlers were able to work regularly and fairly efficiently while using heavily.

The pattern of use was not simply one in which the woman began using intermittently, only to progress to daily use, become increasingly dependent, and perhaps overdose. Rather the pattern that emerged from the interviews was one of intermittent use, use that was sometimes heavy and sometimes light, that included different drugs at various times, and was sometimes of lengthy and sometimes of brief duration. Use was conditioned by patterns of arrest and confinement, income and competing demands on income, availability, psychological state, whim, and the tempo of street life generally.

One factor that seemed to have a very strong effect on problematic usage was relationships with addicted "men" who dealt. Women may have used drugs with their "men" only to have their use become problematic when their "men's" use became problematic or with his arrest or some other tragedy. The most frequent occasion for the step to really problematic use was the arrest, death, or disappearance of a "man," or his rejection of them. Two responses to such an event were typical. On the one hand, a woman then had to provide for her own drug needs while suffering the psychological loss of someone upon whom she was dependent. In this instance, she was likely to hustle indiscriminately and accumulate numerous arrests or an arrest on a serious charge. Betsy's situation, described in detail in Chapter II, illustrates this pattern well. On the other hand, if she had been involved in her "man's" dealing and was regarded as a good risk by his suppliers, his absence might be the occasion for her to take over his business. Eventually, this alternative, too, would lead to arrest. In the meantime, however, the woman had almost unlimited access to drugs and could make a fair amount of money without the immediate risk of apprehension so characteristic of street hustling. The few women who became entrepreneurs in the drug trade did so in ways similar to this. They described these times as their most successful, those of which they were most proud: they were working independently, often took care of their own children, made a reasonable amount of money, and controlled their own supply of drugs. None of this suggests that women who used drugs did not have problems or that it did not contribute to their continued hustling or arrests. It is simply to dispel the myth of the drug-crazed woman hungering for a fix as the typical street woman. Justine, a thirty-year-old white woman with convictions for forgery, fraud, and narcotics trafficking, describes a fairly typical sequence of events this way:

> My daughter wasn't even six months old and we were living together and I had a job and a little welfare on the side and so I kind of had it planned how I was going to make it until the first grade started or whatever the next big change in my life. And I found coming home from work, picking up the kid, going by my ma's or maybe the kid would be with him and the house was a mess and there were three or four people in the kitchen putting needles in their arms and two minutes later, silent, with their heads hanging on the floor. It disgusted me. I'd go to my mother's house and I'd spend days there and I'd end up missing him and coming back yelling and screaming: "What are you doing?" It didn't do any good. And finally one day I just gave in and got high with him. You know, fuck it . . . and going to work high and later to school and coming back and the house was still a mess and they were still there. Fuck it.

Then, Justine's boyfriend overdosed on heroin and died. She was very upset, but determined to get her life in order. She completed her B.A. in Criminal Justice at this time, detoxed off heroin, and got involved in a methadone maintenance program. She landed a job in a drug counseling program but had a serious disagreement with her administrator and was fired. She says she was terminated because she objected to the drug trafficking and use by the staff and clientele at the counseling center. Completely disillusioned, she started to use heroin again. She says:

> I went out and shot around. I needed so much more to overcome the methadone habit that I sold it. I used to deal in an ounce or two ounces a day. That's one to two thousand dollars street money. And from that one to two ounces a day, I might get, oh, three to six grams for myself. Three out of each ounce which would come out to about five hundred dollars street money. So that was my profit for myself. I didn't look for business. Okay? I know, being an opiate user for many years, many other opiate users, you know, and being with my man, so I didn't need to find people to sell to. They were always there and they weren't there for just five or ten dollars' worth; they were there for large amounts. So I didn't have to deal with very many people at all.

Soon, none of Justine's profit was translated into cash, however. It was just the "turn-over" to maintain her habit. Her dealing ended shortly thereafter when someone she had been involved with in forgery set her up (he was an informant for the police) and she was arrested, convicted, and sentenced to three years in Taycheedah.

Clearly, drug use increases the risk of arrest and can influence both the type and the frequency of hustling because it increases the need for fast money. Those women who do develop severe dependencies run the risk of ending up outside of deviant street networks completely because they get defined by other street people as "trouble." They simply are not trustworthy enough to associate with.

Drug use is also associated with poor nutrition and poor health. All of the women who were heavy users had had hepatitis. Drug-related ill health was just one of the many health-related reasons for female street hustlers to withdraw temporarily from street life. Other frequently cited ones were venereal disease, gastrointestinal disorders, pneumonia, and complications of pregnancy.

Health-related reasons that were even more frequently mentioned as occasions for temporary withdrawal from street life than disease or pregnancy included the bruises, broken bones, cuts, and abrasions that were the result of the ever-present risk of violence on the streets. The beatings and sexual assaults female street hustlers received at the hands of their "men," their dates, their wives-in-law, former "women" of their "men," and other street people as well as the police were numerous and often brutal.

Pregnancy itself was a reason for brief spells of inactivity especially among relatively new street hustlers. By the time women had been on the streets for any length of time, however, several bouts of untreated venereal disease had apparently so decreased their fertility that pregnancy rarely occurred. Although these women had fairly large numbers of children for women their age (see Chapter I), then, these children were generally born early in their careers.

By the time they were in their thirties and their children were moving into their teens, the strong link that the care of small children had created between some of these women and their families/households of origin had begun to weaken. The peculiar hold of primary caretakers over female street hustlers also weakened as their careers progressed. One consequence of this was that caretakers often sought custody over the children of female street hustlers at this time, especially during lengthy prison confinements. This sometimes reduced the encumbrances that had limited their participation in street life and pushed them more deeply into it. In addition, they often began to feel deprived of places of refuge to which they could retreat when street life became threatening or wearisome, not so much because they were no longer welcome at home, but because they no longer felt that they belonged there. These primary caretakers themselves were aging and often in ill health and the approaching adolescence of the street hustler's children seemed to indicate, at least within domestic networks, that the dependent status of these women, no matter how limited it had been, was no longer countenanced. Although I have little data on this, it is my hunch that it is soon after this point that female street hustlers really begin to "age out" of street life. They become guardians of their own grandchildren, get straight jobs, and attempt to go to college or pursue some vocational training. There is a certain settling down that I think occurs for these women in their thirties and forties. I have no evidence that some degree of hustling does not continue to be engaged in, however, at least intermittently. The minimal data gathered from the four retired hustlers I interviewed suggests that withdrawal from hustling is rarely complete.

The Everyday Lives of Female Street Hustlers

The everyday lives of the women I interviewed were characterized by alternating periods of hustling and partying; lying low, running, and furtive hustling; ill health or frequent court appearances and institutional confinement; and hustling as outlaw women, independent of street networks. Four discrete categories of behaviors and activities are thus being posed here: "hustlin' and partyin'," "runnin'," "sittin'," and "takin' care of business." A detailed description of the sorts of activities, relationships, and psychological states that predominate during each of the four periods should convey something of the texture of the day-to-day lives of female street hustlers.

"Hustlin' and Partyin'"

The periods of activity that seemed to make street life most attractive to female street hustlers were the periods when they were actively involved with a "man" and, perhaps, several wives-in-law and when the majority of other hustlers with whom they interacted were pulling off scams without being apprehended. Even if they did have the misfortune to be apprehended during such periods, someone had enough money to meet the fine or bail. Several female hustlers recalled the summer of the Bicentennial Celebration as being such a time. One was still quite disappointed at the time of the interview that she was pregnant during the summer of 1976. She said: "I just had to watch the money fly by my hand." In short, periods of hustling and partying are times of fast money for "hungry-money" women.

The women always corrected me when I asked if there was "good money" to be made on the streets. They said that there was, rather, fast money to be made. Although the term fast money obviously denotes money made in a short period of time, it also connotes money made in a "fast" (exciting as opposed to boring) way. Fast money may also be easy money, but that is not its defining characteristic. These women understood that many of them could actually make more money (for their own use) by working a straight job. However, they were also aware that it would still be hard to get by on the money obtained from straight work and that such work would rarely provide them opportunities to feel a sense of mastery, independence, individual accomplishment, and immediate reward. This was how they described feeling, at least some of the time, during periods of hustling and partying. Women were motivated by the desire to feel physically attractive as well. They wanted to have flashy clothes and party with well-dressed "men" who drove long, sleek, late-model automobiles. Women who were outspoken about such desires were referred to as "hungry-money" women.

It was during periods of relatively high living that women who had not previously used hard drugs were most likely to be introduced to their recreational use. When the money was there, members of overlapping deviant street networks might spend several days in a motel room or apartment consuming drugs, ordering out for food, dancing at local hot spots, drinking, and otherwise "gettin' down." On a whim, a "man" and his "women" might simply decide to travel (as opposed to run) to Minneapolis, Memphis, New Orleans, New York, or Miami to continue to hustle and party. For the woman who had been brought up in fairly tight financial circumstances or in a rather sheltered environment or had worked a dead-end job for a while, such a life appeared truly glamorous.

Both their primary caretakers and the female street hustlers themselves referred to this lifestyle, and to its more frequent alternative "runnin'," as "movin' too fast." As compared with either of these alternatives, "sittin'" and "takin' care of business" were spoken of as "slowin' down" or "slowin' down considerably." Although street women would sometimes live in the households in which their children were cared for while running, during periods of hustling and partying, they usually lived with their "man" in a rented room or an apartment. Because they were moving too fast, they only occasionally visited their children during these times if they visited them at all. The money they made was usually appropriated to sustain the partying or to buy luxury items. Those family/household members who cared for their children, even if they were receiving part or all of their AFDC payment, often tried to pressure them to slow down and sometimes took action that ensured that they would slow down. This was less likely to happen if they were sharing the new-found wealth. Georgia described a point during a period of partying and hustling when her drug use was really beginning to become problematic and her uncle intervened:

> I used to snort heroin. I almost had a Jones [addiction] on it where I was gonna go to the needle. I was in the bathroom and I got real cold and I ran out and I started calling people up: "Hey, ya gotta bring me some dope over, now!" And my uncle came in, you know. He's older; he's twenty-eight. And I said: "What's the matter with me?" He said: "You're gonna start shootin' up." He said: "You ride with me." He took me where some junkies was, and I watched these people nod off at the table with needles hanging outta their arms and legs and things, and it just scared me to death.

If women really had slowed down because they had spent several years in Taycheedah, for example, they often expressed feelings of guilt for the way they had treated their children and those who cared for them when they were actively hustling. One woman who was about to be released from Metro Center after having spent over three years in Taycheedah said:

> I'd like to have another child. The one I have, he's eleven, and I was moving too fast when he was growing up. Now, you know, since I've been incarcerated, I've slowed down considerably. I'd like to have a baby, you know, to share a childhood with him. I've missed that terribly. I'm going to be with him now, but he's almost grown.

"Runnin'"

There were several circumstances that could turn hustling and partying into "runnin'" and/or "sittin'." When funds needed to be replenished and "women" and/or their "men" were on the streets flush with the excitement of high living, they seemed less likely to take the usual precautions. Some women referred to being so overcome by greed and so high on the fast life that they were arrested after taking exceptional risks. This sometimes meant committing a crime that was unusual for them, such as an armed robbery, or simply pushing a regular scam too far. If they were not arrested immediately, then, they often knew they were wanted and their lives changed drastically. If they were hot, people they had just spent days with now did not want them around. Depending on the quality of the evidence against them and the seriousness of the crime and its likely penalty, they might run to another state, often with their "man," especially if they had committed the crime in concert. If they were wanted but the charges were not serious or they had nowhere to go and their "man" was not standing by them, chances are they would return home. They would then lie low and hustle furtively without a "man" for protection, bail, or partying. During these times, drug use that had been recreational often became problematic. Women reported being depressed and feeling victimized, hopeless, vulnerable, and disillusioned during periods of running, especially if they were on their own.

Similar reactions were characteristic of "women" who were left behind when their "men" were arrested. As mentioned above, this was sometimes the occasion for a woman to take over her "man's" hustling activity, especially if it was dealing drugs. "Men" generally tried to keep at least the details of their scams from their "women," however, so as to limit the power that such knowledge gave these women over them. A more frequent outcome, then, was depression, anxiety, and increasing dependency on drugs and alcohol. Whether the woman returned home often depended on where she was at the time and what her own legal status was.

This was the usual sequence of events unless the woman could immediately link up with another "man." There were several things that might interfere with this. She might feel a commitment to or fear of her most recent "man" and not want or dare to betray him. Other well-established "men" might be afraid to take her on for similar reasons or because she herself was hot. The current "women" of a potential "man" might make it clear that another wife-in-law would simply not be tolerated. The prevalent tendency among the women interviewed who had sustained a relationship with a family/household of origin was for them to return home.

During periods of running, a woman might hustle with other "women" and/or pull off scams with family/household members who were involved in "the life." Although the idea was to get involved only in relatively safe scams during this period, the quest for drugs and their consumption could put a woman in a situation where she had no choice but to hustle alone because no one would hustle with her and where her consumption of drugs heightened her risk of additional arrests. Moreover, concern about her drug use and general safety made primary caretakers in her family/household of origin likely during these times, as during times of hustling and partying, either to be unwilling to rescue her when she had a run-in with the law or to deliberately arrange her arrest. There was also the fact that caretakers were getting a first-hand view of the seamier side of street life as it affected one of their own. They were confronted head-on with something most of them had explicitly not wanted for their female charges. In addition, during such times, they were unlikely to receive what they thought was an adequate contribution to the running of the household at the same time that they were probably being put upon by the woman's mere presence, her everyday personal need for money, and her need for money as a result of her drug use and her contacts with the law. Unless a female street hustler linked up with another "man," then, running inevitably led to sitting.

"Sittin'"

There were several varieties of sitting. Apart from temporary withdrawal from street life due to ill health, the most usual variety of sitting is done in the Milwaukee County Jail or the Milwaukee County House of Correction. While so confined, street women talked among themselves about their scams and planned how to pull them off without being apprehended in the future. Although the women in both institutions were supposedly segregated from the men, there was frequent contact. Women enlarged their contacts with deviant network members while confined and often met their future "men" in prison. Otherwise, unless the women were released daily on Huber Law, sitting involved just that. Except for meals, exercise, and occasional crafts, religious services, and drug and alcohol counseling, they sat and watched television or chatted all day. No reading materials or educational instruction are available.

The one thing that clearly was accomplished during these periods was the curtailment of drug use. At the House of Correction, a drug counseling program was available, but more important, "urine screens" were done daily on women known to have histories of drug use and on all inmates who were bussed into Milwaukee on Huber Law. Drugs were available for those with the money to buy them, but except for an occasional shared joint, the women interviewed did not have access to harder drugs or were afraid to use them. The penalty for a positive screen was solitary confinement. As a result, when the woman returned to the streets, she had reduced drug requirements.

Women who had done their sitting at Taycheedah tended to be older and more advanced in their careers. They had also committed more serious crimes and were imprisoned for years rather than months. These women had received some training while in prison and most had received their GEDs while incarcerated. Like the women in jail or the House of Correction, these females had contacts with males who would occasionally become their "men" upon release. Some married "men" while in prison. Hustling for them in the near future at least would probably be very low-key. The experience of being in prison for such a long time did have an effect. They still spoke of having slowed down considerably; however, they had no term for completely withdrawing from street life. My sense is that many of them never do.

"Takin' Care of Business"

Only rarely did especially self-confident women, women really quite atypical of those interviewed, describe attempts to hustle as outlaw women, completely independent of "men." This usually occurred after they had been badly victimized by a "man" they really cared for. All of the women who attempted solo hustling of this sort did so only once. Only women who were relatively free of legal encumbrances, or were new to the streets and did not know any better, freely chose solo hustling. It was, then, a sort of stand for independence, for taking charge of one's life. Women said of such times: "I just decided nobody knows how to spend my money better than me." Because such decisions were clearly made with a larger referent than simply street activity, such moves often also involved moving into an apartment of one's own and taking responsibility for the care of one's children. These decisions were sometimes portrayed to family/household members as the first steps in efforts to slow down and, as such, were both applauded and looked upon with skepticism.

This phase of hustling behavior was, like hustling and partying, short-lived. "Men" would simply not permit women to hustle in this fashion. In addition, the care of children is incompatible with street hustling. One woman described her attempt to hustle solo and its failure as follows:

> I ran away from my "man" 'cause he beat me, but he found me and I went back. And then I got a case for prostitution. They brought me in. And, you know, he let me sit in jail. That's when I kind of got away from him. He let me just sit, and I know he had the money 'cause I had just made a sting. I came in late with somethin' like fifteen hundred dollars. I thought I was rich. He said: "Is this all you got?" And he told me to get dressed and go back out. And me, like a dummy, I mean that I was, at the time, I got dressed and went back out and caught a case for solicitin'. And then I called him, and he said: "Where you at?" "You know where I'm at; I'm in jail." "For what?" Like he had no idea. And so he knew that, too. And at that time they were trying to bust all the pimps. I said I was gonna tell on him. So, he said he'd be down the next day to get me out. I didn't want to stay overnight, but I didn't have much choice. He didn't come the next day, or the next day, or the next day. By the time I got out, I was pretty mad, and I decided I didn't need me no "man." I was just out hustlin'. I thought I would show them. I would take my son. I'm going to be the mother, you know, this whole trip. It didn't work out like that. I was still movin' too fast. I ended up taking my son back and forth to my foster-mother almost daily. On my own, I didn't work as a prostitute. I was forgin'. But, still, I ran into a lot of fellas that used to try and terrorize me. They just tried to force themselves on me. It just didn't work.

A complex set of factors, then, influences the shape and direction of a female street hustler's life during her most active working years, the period from her mid to late teens to her late twenties. Her relationships with kinspersons and "men," contacts with the criminal justice system, fertility and general health, physical attractiveness, drug or alcohol use, and responsibility for children all have separate and interacting effects. Conversely, her involvement in illegal work has a feedback effect in that it may also influence some of the aforementioned characteristics and relationships.

What is being described is a self-contained and, indeed, self-perpetuating world of illegal work. The only major force that eventually pushes some women out into the straight world is age. There is some evidence, however, that even "women" who appear at first glance to be rather well-integrated into the world of school and/or legitimate work frequently keep one foot firmly planted in the fast life. It is in a very real sense more secure and familiar to them that the straight world is or may ever become.

CHAPTER
VI
Dreams: Aspirations, Role Models, and Attitudes

The worldview of the female street hustlers interviewed in Milwaukee is a melange of interpretations, rationalizations, and idealizations based upon their own experiences and taken-for-granted notions about what is good and proper for women generally, women like themselves, and significant others. These notions seem to derive from the curious intermingling of straight and street cultures to which they have been exposed. Despite a range of individual experiences and backgrounds, certain ideational patterns are detectable in women who have been involved in deviant street networks for any length of time.

The beliefs of Milwaukee street women cannot be portrayed as a set of neatly interlocking and compatible ideas. Nor are behaviors of group members always consistent with expressed beliefs. Rather, the ideas and actions in question sometimes appear, at least to the outsider, as mutually exclusive or, at the very least, antagonistic. What seems to be a hard and fast rule that derives from a heartfelt belief is modified or negated in an instant because such rules generally are situationally and, at times, opportunistically malleable. These ideas have an impact on day-to-day behavior and, to the degree that they shape the perception of possible options for the future, affect long-range planning (or account for its absence). For this reason, it is important to consider the worldview of the female street hustlers interviewed. To this end, I will discuss three different ideational indicators of worldview: aspirations, role models, and selected attitudes. The complex interplay of action and thought will be examined. Of particular interest are those ideational elements that would indicate the presence of social-psychological forces that reinforce, counter, or explain the structuring of the street woman's world already examined.

Aspirations

Occupational and Related Aspirations

Regardless of origin, a large number of the women I interviewed said that as children they wanted to be nurses. Most other career choices were also stereotypically female ones: daycare worker, airline stewardess, social worker. The women also chose occupations that were familiar to them as children, ones where they recalled actually seeing women perform the duties associated with the particular occupation. It is interesting that, although teaching would also appear to be a very likely choice, none of these women recalled wanting to be teachers. It is possible that because they generally did not do well in school and because school was often, rather, the setting for conflict and failure, teachers were not conceived of in especially positive terms. Alternatively, teaching itself might have been conceived of as an occupation for which they were unlikely to have the requisite skills.

The majority of these women also fantasized about getting married and having children of their own, but most of them thought that they would work outside the home themselves at least part-time or after their children entered school. They overwhelmingly rejected the lives of their mothers or female guardians as models for their own. Whether their own mother combined occupational therapy, factory work, or janitorial work with homemaking, or worked outside the home not at all, they did not want to have lives like their mothers'. They saw their mothers' lives as filled with drudgery and disappointment, as the epitome of boredom. Minority women especially were likely to feel that their mothers just had had too many children to allow themselves or their children quality lives. This is not to say that they condemned them for this state of affairs, but rather to say that theirs were not lives they wished to emulate.

The female street hustlers I interviewed, with the exception of those one would classify as pushouts, also recalled that their parents or guardians encouraged them to pursue occupations like the ones they fantasized about. Many could not remember whether their choice was originally their own or their parents' or guardians'. Even if those in charge of these women did not suggest or actively initiate conversations about particular occupations, the women recalled their emphasizing the importance of education for future employability. Graduating from high school at the very least was stressed as something to be seriously and diligently pursued.

At the same time that these girls were having dreams about occupations they thought more exciting than those of their mothers, many of them were being exposed to the world of illegal work. For them, the work of women whose occupations placed them within this alternative world had a certain reality and immediacy lacking in the work of nurses or social workers. Rosemary, a twenty-year-old black woman, talks about one of her early contacts with the glamour associated with the streets:

Maybe one day I'll be a famous dancer. I go-go dance. Maybe if I keep on doin' and doin' it, if I keep on, 'cause I like to dance, and, ah . . . oh, when I, uh, was fourteen, I wanted to be a go-go girl. 'Cause the lady that use to live across the street, she use to dance all the time. And she used to show me different things that I knew how to do when I was little. And I thought she was, you know, she had on a big, pretty wig, and she just looked pretty, you know? I liked her style. She knew how to dress and that, and she could dance.

Concepcion, a twenty-three-year-old woman of Puerto Rican descent, recalls childhood dreams and plans that reveal competing legal and illegal occupational models:

I seen plenty bloodshed, fights, rumbles, and things like that. Heard 'bout killin' all day long, right next door, right on our sidewalk, you know? Damn, you know, I used to look right outta my window, right on "the stroll" [sidewalk used by prostitutes to attract customers]. And, ah, I use to say: "Look at all those prostitutes," you know? "Damn, I can do that."

When you were a child, what did you think life would be like when you were all grown up?

I thought it was gonna be, ah, really sharp, you know? I couldn't wait to be of age.

What did you think you were going to be?

I thought I was gonna work. Woah, I had plenty ideas, you know? I wanted to be a nurse, you know, simple things like that, you know? There's one thing I really wanted to do and that was to travel. I always imagined myself, and I was always carryin' travelin' bags, you know? I would get my travelin' bag and stuff it and go downtown, and just go all over the place. I wanted to do . . . thought, you know, I'd become part of the "jet set."

Yolanda, another Puerto Rican woman, gives us some insight into how much such women typically lack in information about the nature of higher education and the credentialing relevant to particular career goals:

When I was little I was, uh, I always got off into the law, you know? And I always wanted to be an attorney because I have, you know, like if I feel like something's right, I get, what is it? real radical, or political, or whatever, and I'm still like that, you know? And I've always wanted to be an attorney, you know, always. And my father, he always told me: "Go ahead; go ahead," you know? And he said that if I would, he would be so proud of me. And if I would go to college, he would buy me a car, which I kinda wanted, and all this stuff, you know? But I never made it. I am going to college now.

Oh? What one are you attending?

American Beauty College of Prestige.

Many of the women who spoke about plans to go to college meant just the sort of college Yolanda was attending. Often, when pressed, they knew very little about what was involved. One young black woman was quite shocked and indignant when she inadvertently learned from me that one had to pay money to go to college.

Women who had had lengthy confinements in jail or prison were likely to have completed GEDs and to have better information about how they might actually pursue particular occupations. Greater exposure to the criminal justice system also meant that women added to the list of desirable occupations such occupations as drug counselor, probation officer, parole officer, and correctional administrator. It was the firm belief of these women that someone who had actually experienced street life and the criminal justice system could do a better job than those who now were likely to hold such positions.

Although social class of family and, indeed, individual experiences seem to have had little impact on the legitimate occupations these women say they aspired to as children, the experience of having been confined in Taycheedah did seem to broaden their options as adults. Women who had been sent to Taycheedah for a lengthy stay upon a felony conviction had, without exception, completed their GEDs and had usually received additional vocational or academic training as well. As a result of recent criticism, Wisconsin and other states have instituted training in non-traditional careers for women who are interested. Thus, along with training in tailoring, typing, cosmetology, shorthand, and data processing, inmates can take courses in areas such as auto mechanics. They can also learn to be machinists. Several of the women I interviewed had, in fact, taken such courses.

Apart from the often insurmountable problems that any woman would have in trying to enter such male-dominated occupations, the women interviewed who had such training were highly unlikely to pursue jobs of this sort anticipatory to release or afterwards because they had such very conventional ideas with regard to gender-appropriate work. Diane, a black woman of twenty-seven who had spent thirty-nine months in Taycheedah for forgery, had had training in keypunching in high school and had actually worked for eleven months as a keypuncher before she had become involved in street life. She said of that time:

It was, you know, the work isn't hard and I'm pretty fast, but it was very boring . . . just watching those cards go by all day and punching them, all day. It was very boring. I'd rather be in a factory. I was working at Sears' warehouse. And I applied for the position of working in the clothing department. They asked me for experience, and I put down keypunch training. But that's not the kinda job I wanted. The thing they really needed was a keypuncher, though. And now I'm going to be an auto mechanic/beautician [her eyes twinkle and she laughs].

When I asked her to explain, Diane told me that she had received her beautician's license while in Taycheedah and also her certificate in auto mechanics. Her aim, she says, is to direct her own daycare center, however. She wanted, above all, the freedom of being her own boss. She didn't want to be a beautician because she didn't think that she could get the capital together to open her own shop. She explained that doing people's hair in one's own home was illegal. She thought she might be able to start her own daycare center, however. When I asked her about being an auto mechanic, she replied:

I don't think about doing that much. Ah, car mechanics unless I get into the muffler part, the rest of it is too messy. I can do tune-ups without getting too dirty, but when I start messin' with grease jobs and shocks, then grease gets all over, on my hands, under my finger nails. The way your nails look, you look like a mechanic. I don't want that.

Anita, a black woman of twenty-three who had also been in Taycheedah, was working as a machine operator in a plastics factory at the time of the interview. I asked her if she liked her job and she said:

No! I mean it's terrible, you know, 'cause like when I be really going at it, you know, it seems like I be doin' a man's work. Though I went to school for machinist and it pays some nice money, but it's not what I want to do because I also get, you know; okay, I took up typing, you know. I could type. I could be a secretary or typing, but then that

don't bring in enough money for me, you know? So, I
wanted this job, you know, not because I like it, but because
I'm gonna need it. I'll keep it until I can take a day off to
look for another job.

The sorts of legitimate jobs that these women want, then,
are stereotypically female jobs, but jobs that are also glamorous,
exciting, and offer a degree of independence. The number of
women who told me that if they could have any occupation they
wanted, they would be performers, that is, singers or dancers, was
truly astonishing. As a matter of fact, later in Diane's interview,
in response to a question about what sorts of women she admired,
she said:

> Most of the people I admire are people that I feel I could get
> into that area like. Have you ever watched this disco pro-
> gram on television? Well, they have this dancer on there,
> and her name is Fire. And you don't ever see her face. If she
> watched for herself, she would never recognize herself. I say:
> "I could do that." I'd go in, and I'd make myself a costume.
> They wouldn't ever forget my face. I love to dance. But, you
> know, if you're gonna be a go-go dancer, you gonna always
> associate with just the riff-raff and stuff. But if you . . . Lola
> Falana, she's a dancer, and she made it. I just wonder:
> "When is my turn?" I want to be like Lola Falana. Some-
> body should discover me. I've been around all these years
> and no one has discovered me yet. But they will; somewhere
> they will. I'm gonna get some recognition. If I can't get into,
> you know, *The Guiness Book of Records* for forgery, maybe
> I'll get it for the daycare center.

The topic of occupational aspirations is additionally con-
fusing because none of the women I interviewed, even those who
have been released after lengthy periods in Taycheedah, rule out
illegal work altogether for the future. This finding is, of course,
partially a function of my snowball sampling method. I interviewed primarily women who were active street hustlers. Women
who may have dropped out of the world of illegal work along the
way were not interviewed. It is interesting to note, however, that
all four of the retired female street hustlers I interviewed still

engage in some illegal work on the side to supplement their incomes, which are generally quite small, deriving as they do from such sources as General Assistance, disability, and state vocational rehabilitation programs.

There are several factors that keep the female street hustlers I interviewed hustling and prevent them from entering or even attempting to enter the world of legal work. First, they lack the requisite skills and information about what those skills are and how they might be acquired. Second, they generally believe that there are some occupations that are simply incompatible with their perceptions of themselves as women. Third, what they would really like are glamorous jobs, but jobs that are glamorous in a way distinct from the way in which a female attorney's job might be thought of as glamorous. These women think that ideally they would like jobs where their physical attributes, those attributes that have been at least partially responsible for their financial survival in the past, would really get their due. At the level that most of them are able to pursue careers as performers, however, one finds exactly the same sort of deviant network connections with which they have been involved in the past. Fourth, they desire work that gives them a good deal of freedom and independence. Jobs for which they are likely to qualify, even non-traditional jobs that might offer substantial monetary rewards, are unlikely to offer these other sorts of benefits as well. Money was not often mentioned as a reason to dream about pursuing a particular line of work. They may assume that the sorts of jobs about which they fantasize would pay them highly or they may assume that the skills they have developed on the streets will always allow them to supplement their incomes should they need to. My hunch is that the explanation lies in some combination of the two.

For reasons enumerated above, then, these women do not sever their ties with deviant street networks. They remain vulnerable to exploitation by the men who control these networks and are unable even to conceive of themselves as ever completely withdrawing.

It is important to note that whereas in the preceding chapters I have been discussing structural constraints that lead to the recruitment of young women to "the life" and to their continued participation in it, such as exposure to deviant street networks and decreasing commitment to relationships with non-network members, here I am talking about parallel social-psychological constraints. These are partially generated by the occupational aspirations of these women. They are complicated by their values with regard to relationships with the opposite sex and family life.

Relational Aspirations

Although some of the women interviewed made mention of homosexual alliances forged while imprisoned at Taycheedah and homosexual acts performed for pay while on the streets, only one woman defined herself as a lesbian. When asked to think about the sort of familial arrangements they would like for themselves and their children in the future, the responses were once again stereotypic. They wanted to own homes in which they could raise their children in comfort. Most of all, they wanted men who would be faithful to them and who would take care of them.

Georgia is a black woman of twenty-one who has been in Taycheedah for manslaughter and also has convictions for numerous property offenses. She has two children. A third disappeared under very mysterious circumstances. My hunch, from speaking with her and with others, is that she sold the child. Formal charges were never filed in the case, however. Georgia had the following to say in this regard:

> I do want a husband. I want a man to take care of me, who will accept my children like they were his. I want . . . just like to go to work and come back, fix supper, do my little home care around the house, whatever needs to be done. Then, maybe, sit down and play a game with my kids and my husband or sit down and watch TV with the family. Somethin' different. Things that I never done in my life, you know.

The problem with this dream is that, with the exception of their dates, these women have little contact with straight men. In fact, most of them do not believe that straight men would be able to relate to them. The general feeling is that straight men would be so square that they would be sexually unattractive and down-

right boring. A black minister, who is a Ph.D. candidate at the
university at which I teach and whose church is in a section of the
city from which many of the women interviewed come, suggested
that the women may voice these objections because they themselves are so stigmatized among straight men in their own communities. I have no way of knowing whether or not this is the
case; however, it certainly seems plausible.

Possibly it is too cynical to assume that a street woman and a
street man could not have a straight life together. It seems highly
unlikely, however, for several reasons. If they remain in the city in
which they engaged in the illegal work of deviant street networks,
their connections with others in those networks and sometimes
their own domestic networks will draw them back to hustling.
They do not have the personal skills that will allow them to have
the style of life they envision by working solely in legitimate jobs
they are likely to get, even with further training.

While she was a prisoner at Taycheedah, Diane married a
prisoner at Waupun who was doing time for armed robbery.
Interviewed at Metro Center, an arm of Taycheedah in Milwaukee, she said:

> I married him a year ago in June. He was the first man . . . I
> met him right after I got outta Oregon . . . and he was the
> first man I had met that wanted to take care of me. We lived
> together for about eight months. We was kinda playing at
> married at that time. He couldn't marry me. He didn't have
> his divorce yet. He went to jail for six years for armed rob-
> bery . . . when he was in jail and I was free, we weren't
> married. So, I felt, you know, well, he's in jail . . . as long
> as, you know, I stick close to him and take care of his little
> needs and stuff, he shouldn't get too uptight. So, I did mess
> around. But now we're married. I don't want him to mess
> around. And he's been out since the beginning of the year.
> It's time for me to go home and see what kind of relation-
> ship we have. Every time he comes to see me, I say: "What's
> her name?" And he says: "It's not like that, sugar. I have no
> woman now." But I don't trust him.

So, is there another woman?

There was at one time. He said: "You really want to know?"
I said: "I really want to know." He said: "It's really nothin'
serious." I said: "Is she pretty?" He said: "No, she's ugly
with false teeth and warts." I know she is pretty, and I don't
want him to mess around with her.

Apart from all the factors listed above that militate against
such a couple living a straight life, then, a level of distrust so
colors these unions that the relationships themselves are often not
very long-lived. Diane's later comments, also quite typical of
those voiced by street women, shed even more light on her vision
of the relationship.

Has he got a straight job?

He's a welder. I wish he was a trucker. That's more money.

Welders make pretty good money, don't they?

Yeah, I guess. Truckers get more, I think.

Yeah, but they're away.

I know [laughs]. Then I could go out more. I think he
thinks. . . . He's in for a big surprise. I know he's gonna
think that as soon as I get outta jail, I'm gonna stay at home.
I'm not. I didn't want to stay at home before. I like to go out.
He's probably gonna be gone more than he's home. I'm not
gonna be alone. I said: "Why don't you be a trucker?" I
won't stay at home. I need to dance. I used to always tell him
when I was in prison . . . I used to always say: "When I get
out, I'm gonna dance. I'm gonna meet a buncha nice people." He said: "You just want to get back into the same
thing you did before." I said: "No, I don't." He said: "Who
do you think you're talkin' to? I knows you. You don't
really needs to dance." I do, though.

The last reason why these relationships are unlikely to last
with both partners working straight jobs is that when and if

employment becomes problematic, street income is an easy, if risky, solution. Because sexual attractiveness is such a key to success in that world, however, unless the couple participates in hustling together, the very sexual nature of the work often undercuts a monogamous model. In addition, because men in our culture become dignified with age, while women just become old, it is my hypothesis that if these women remain in the cities in which they were active in street life, they end up alone and/or in situations very similar to those of the women who mothered them. Men, on the other hand, can, for much longer periods of time, be the beneficiaries of the illegal work of younger women.

Role Models

When female street hustlers talked about women in public life whom they would like to be like or particularly admired, they tended to choose performers, very wealthy women, or politically active women of color. Choices such as Della Reese, Raquel Welch, Eva Gabor, Donna Summer, Natalie Cole, Cicely Tyson, Jackie Onassis, Coretta Scott King, Billie Holiday, Nancy Wilson, and Angela Davis were common.

They had a difficult time when asked if there were women they actually knew whom they regarded with great respect or wished they were like. Some mentioned women who were able to turn tricks or sell drugs discretely, had a dedicated "man," and seemed to be doing very well financially. Many reported having heard about women who made a great deal of money on the street and now lived lives of leisure as a result of their wise investments. If such women existed, no one seemed to know any of them personally. Rumor had it that there was a ball held yearly at a mansion in the country by and for street women and their "men." The description I heard of this event made it sound incredibly elegant with groups arriving by limousine and then consuming endless glasses of champagne. The men reportedly wore tuxedos; the women gowns and furs. Jewelry adorned both males and females. The partying continued through the weekend. Several women wanted to be like the women who went to this mythical ball. However, again, no one seemed to know anyone who had attended such an event.

With the exception of those women who spoke of the

accomplishments of black women identified with the civil rights movement, the women singled out for emulation were overwhelmingly performers and women of wealth. Such women were often the choice of non-minority women as well. White women were most likely to choose women independently involved in illegal work and straight women as women they would like to be like. My belief is that the general tendency described here reflects the degree to which these women had relationships with deviant street network members almost to the exclusion of all others.

These role models are consistent with the occupational and marital aspirations of the women. Female street hustlers tended to choose as role models public figures who were glamorous, wealthy, and projected a certain sensuousness. These were women who they felt were somehow successful versions of themselves, who embodied what they might become, if given the chance. Similarly, the women they actually knew and admired did what they did, only more successfully. Since success is very fleeting for most women involved in the illegal work of the streets, the women interviewed were hard put when asked to actually single out such women. They had to resort to women they had once heard about, women who probably only existed in fantasy. Except for female civil rights leaders, very few women said they wanted to be like straight women they knew or knew of. A few women mentioned admiring their own mothers for certain of their personal strengths and qualities, but none of them wished they could be like them. By and large, these women simply did not know the straight women with whom they were acquainted well enough to want to be like them nor did they know enough about the straight world of the professional woman to find it attractive. What they did know seemed boring and pedestrian compared to the glamour of the lives of performers and even the occasional glitter of their own.

Attitudes

The Women's Movement and Women Generally

My initial interest in the topic of female street hustlers was, as described in Chapter I, aroused by the arguments made by researchers such as Freda Adler (1975) and Rita James Simon

(1975) who claimed that recent increases in the criminality of women might be linked to the latest manifestation of the women's movement. Although the purpose of this work is obviously not to test that link but rather to investigate in some depth the social world of street women (and street women living in a moderate-sized midwestern city at that), it has become more and more clear that the increases that have occurred in the criminality of women have been in those areas—prostitution, larceny (shoplifting), forgery, and fraud (credit-card)—where street women are most likely to be active (Steffensmeier 1980). Given that fact, I thought it might be informative to ask these women some questions about the women's movement.

Although their information about the movement and their support for it varies quite predictably with their education, almost all are poorly educated (see Chapter I) and, thus, know very little about the movement. They neither share its assumptions about the nature of society and the current position of women in it nor support its strategies for change. They do believe that women should receive equal pay for equal work and that women should be allowed to do "men's work" if they want to and are qualified, but they also believe that men and women are naturally designed and suited for different sorts of work, social roles, and statuses. My questions about the movement itself elicited some responses that were memorable. For example, there was: "The ERA? Isn't that a band that came to play at Taycheedah?" or "I like real feminist women like Raquel Welch and Eva Gabor."

Moreover, if the street women interviewed distrust individual men, they distrust women as a group even more. Again and again, women told me that they had few, if any, female friends and that women, generally, were "snitch-bitches." Women are seen as jealous, gossipy troublemakers who are both more emotional and less rational than men. There is, of course, a great deal of competition among them for good "men" and they often undercut each other's attempts to sustain relationships with "men." The "men" themselves often instigate conflicts among their "women" and other street women as well in order to control them more easily. Thus, the experiences street women are likely to have had with other street women lead them at least in part to come to the conclusions they do about the nature of women. Diane made a revealing comment in this regard:

They're jealous. I don't understand it. But, then, I never dealt with women too much on the street. I had a group of just one or two female friends that I would normally go out with. And the rest of them were men I had known over the years. And I could sit with men and just talk. I couldn't say that about a lot of female friends. We would be partyin' and the next thing you knew this woman would try to steal my "man." That's enough right there for me to really hurt somebody. I caught my friend one time in bed with my "man." I was mad enough to want to kill them both, but, instead, I jumped on her. Women are just so petty. They gossip and make trouble. Men don't. Women bring something up to have a grudge, you know? They argue about it, and every time they see you after it, they say, "You bitch." And it's all because of the same thing. They never discuss it. They just hide behind it. There's no discussin' with a mad woman. She just won't think reasonable and logical. I know 'cause when I get mad, I won't.

As Diane suggests, if women do have female friends, they are usually few in number. These friends are often women one runs with, sometimes referred to as "running partners." The use of the term "running" here suggests, I think, that these are women who have either proved their loyalty in a stressful or threatening situation (when one is running) or could be expected to do so. For all of the reasons enumerated above, few women have female running partners because, although by their very nature a bit more resistant to the stresses of street life than relationships with other women, these relationships too are eventually undermined by "men" or by the episodic nature of the female street hustler's life.

There is, then, little sense of camaraderie among female street hustlers, little sense of political identification with women generally. It became very clear to me that minority and non-minority women alike were much more likely to define their own personal problems in terms of racial prejudice and discrimination or general social inequality than in terms of sexual inequality.[1]

1. This finding is consistent with those of Gurin (1985) for U.S. women generally. She found that except for strong criticism of the legitimacy of gender disparities in the labor force, women's gender consciousness was comparatively weak. Gender was found to be a weaker basis of political consciousness than age, social class, or race.

And, given the middle-class nature of the women's movement, at least as it is most likely to reach the public through the news media, the question of their "liberation" just does not seem to be the first question one should ask when one attempts to speak of ameliorating the lives of female street hustlers. In short, the women's movement of *Ms. Magazine* has not touched them.

Why I Do What I Do

When asked about why they hustle, street women give a variety of answers. Some say for the excitement; others say for the money; and still others seem to think that they are innately evil, controlled by something beyond themselves. Very often they said: "The life just gets in your blood." When asked why a particular woman got involved in an especially dangerous and foolhardy undertaking or why women generally got involved in deviant street networks, however, they were unanimous in saying that it was because of some "man." Rosemary described her motive as follows:

> I like the excitement. It's dangerous, I guess, but you meet different people. I just relate, you know, I relate to people better who are in "the life". . . because . . . ah, like a square girl, what do they talk about? Nothin'! "Oh, my boyfriend's this and that." I think it's boring. I like to talk about somethin' excitin', about . . . like money and how she went about getting the money. Then I'll know the next time how to get it better. It's just a game. That's all it is. I realize it. It's not going to last forever. But, shit, I'm enjoyin' it while I'm doin' it.

On the other hand, Julie, a surly black woman with convictions for prostitution and shoplifting, was indignant at my questioning her motives. She came from a desperately poor home and, when asked why she did what she did, she shot back angrily;

> For the money . . . because I needed it. Evidently whatever it was I was doin' wasn't too much from the start. I mean, you'd get out and figure, nothin' happened that time. I did it 'cause I had to. I mean 'cause my mother couldn't do it,

and my daddy was a dog, and that's all I can say. So, when I look back, I say he was a dog because she couldn't make no money. She had too many babies. I just had to; I still do.

Among those who think that the street life is somehow "in their blood" or that something beyond them somehow "makes them do" what they do are Yolanda and Georgia. Yolanda's response to my query about whether or not she thought it likely that she'd get out of "the life" was:

Yes, sometime I will . . . well, then, it's in my blood, too. But, if I was to have, um, someone special that didn't want me to be in "the life," and . . . well, maybe he wouldn't know that I was in "the life," you know? And, ah, or maybe just mellow it out. Be mellow with the person I'm fond of, very fond of. Then if he was to find out that I was in "the life," it would hurt him. I wouldn't want that. If he was really good to me, I might take a crack at it [quitting].

For Georgia, participation in street life is due to something mysterious that resides within her. It's not just a matter of having become habituated to a particular style of life. She described the time just prior to her incarceration in Taycheedah as follows:

I was really bad then, you know. It's still in me and I want it to come out. It seems like at times I'm just possessed. I don't know . . . or it's just a lotta strain on the brain. I just don't know. It would be very hard for me to live a straight life. I'm cold. I have a temper. With me temptation is always out there waiting. I'm really serious. I know how this sounds, but, um, in prison I used to sit and plot how I was gonna get the girls' money out of their accounts. Do you believe it? And if they . . . I probably woulda got into trouble if they woulda released me from Taycheedah because I had already, you know, planned a way how to drain everybody's account there without no one knowing what happened. So, you see my mind is constantly. . . . And so since I been locked up, all I had time to do was think about good things in life, how to be wiser. A person'd have to be possessed. Deep down inside I believe I have a problem. I'm beyond the point where anybody can reach me. I'm a money fanatic.

Whatever the expressed motivation for their individual involvement in deviant street networks, these women agree on one thing. Men are involved. Rosemary describes the general feeling very well:

> The reason most womens does crimes is mens. I think it's more prostitutes, you know. Everybody's gettin' into the street life. Everybody's runnin' around. He's a pimp; she's a whore. And, then, you know, older brothers . . . 'cause my "man," he tells his brother, you know, how to talk to girls to get their money, how to talk them into going on the streets. So, I think that's what it is 'cause it's . . . there's a lot of 'em now. Young girls, too. I know a lot of 'em, you know, that want . . . that need me to take 'em, you know, places where they can get some money. And I took one before, but, ah, I just told her: "Whatever you do, don't keep on doin' this 'cause once it's in your blood, it stays there forever; you just get it in your bloodstream." You just know you can get the money; you gonna go on out and get it. So, I think it's just more mens influencin' womens.

What It Takes to Be a Street Woman

A phrase I heard frequently as I came to know more and more of Milwaukee's female street hustlers was "having the knowledge of money" or simply "having the wisdom." After hearing it used in different contexts and asking about it, my conclusion is that "having the wisdom" refers to a particular set of qualities and skills that make a "good" (successful) street woman. Primary among them is the ability to maipulate people or "con" people into giving you their money without resorting to violence. If you're good at what you do, the implication is that this can be accomplished without having to give much of yourself in return. Ideally the "mark" (the person targeted for a hustle) should not feel conned but that he or she has done only what he or she should have. For example, a street woman who is being paid for sex and is able to get the money (perhaps more money than was originally agreed upon) without living up to her part of the bargain would be said to have the wisdom. A woman with the wisdom would, in turn, not allow herself to be conned. Female street hustlers used the term to describe women who knew right away when they got

into the car with a prospective date or started a conversation with
one in a tavern whether or not the man was with the vice squad.
The term was also used to describe women who could distinguish
"good men" from "men" who "weren't nothin' but pimps."
Women were so often duped in this regard, however, and were so
hurt and mortified when it occurred, that bad judgment did not
seem to disqualify them from having the wisdom. For a street
woman to suggest this would surely initiate a fight. Mildred describes these problems of judgment:

> I worked for city hall, for the police department and every-
> thing. That's how I met him. He was walkin' across the
> street one day. Yup, and he walked against me. [She was
> working as a crossing guard.] And I said: "Where do you
> think you're goin'? Hey, I cross people here." He said: "I
> don't need anyone to cross me." I said: "Yes, you do. Just
> stay 'til the sign says 'walk,' not 'don't walk.'" He must
> have said: "And who does this bitch think she is?" I see him
> walk across the street. I say to myself: "I'm gonna get him
> when he comes back." I waited for him and said: "Come and
> cross now." He said: "I'm not gonna cross there. Why do
> you have to charge me, baby? Don't charge me." When he
> said that, I wondered: "What is he tellin' me, don't charge
> him? Does he think he is some 'player' [street man, pimp] or
> somethin'? He ain't gonna play on me." So, ever since then,
> I would say when I saw him: "Don't charge me, baby; you're
> still chargin' me, yea; walk with the light." So he just
> started . . . it took him three months to approach me, from
> June to October. When he did, I said: "When you gonna
> take me out with all your money?" I be thinkin' he was a
> good old mark. Then I approach him with another perspec-
> tive. I approach him with giving loving, tender care and
> affection, which I figured he needed. And he did. He was so
> vulnerable when I first met him, he gave me everything.
> And, um, that's why I say I have the knowledge of money, I
> have the wisdom. I knew how to get it. All I did was talk. It's
> getting over the system. I've learned how to get over banks,
> how to get over people. In the end, you hurt people, and
> sometimes you get hurt yourself, but you have to know how
> to have it.

The double-edged effect of having the wisdom revealed in the last sentence of Mildred's statement was something that was not lost on any of the women interviewed. It caused them, for example, to react ambivalently to any indication that their own children might be developing the wisdom. This ambivalence is obvious in the following statement by Diane:

> I hope one day my little girl will be able to be something I wasn't able to be. I don't want her to be like me. She's like me now 'cause she demands things. She gets . . . you wouldn't believe it . . . that a little seven-year-old. . . . I kind of admire her. But for one thing I always tell her I want her to go to college, you know, be somebody. Like I always tell her a high school diploma don't mean anything. I don't care if you do get it. It don't mean anything. I want her to go to college. I don't want her to . . . she always wants . . . you know what she says? "I'm going to be just like my mother. My mother's fast." You know it just makes me sick to hear her say that. And then she run around conning. She run around conning my aunt and uncle, you know. She, um, she made 'em buy her a bike and she made 'em buy her a watch on Saturday and one for her brother, too. Then she turned around and got a gold necklace. I mean what does a seven-year-old do with a forty-seven-dollar necklace? You tell me.

Having the knowledge of money or the wisdom was a sign of professional status among these women, then; it was a body of knowledge and skill that set them apart from other women in other occupations. It was felt that women who had the wisdom would always be able to make a living, even after they were no longer active in street life. It was something for a woman "to fall back on" when she was without a man to take care of her. The feeling that one has the wisdom, then, keeps the door to illegal work open even for those women who no longer actively participate in deviant street networks.

The Law

One might assume that repeated encounters with the criminal justice system would undermine a street woman's confidence that she has the wisdom. This occurs sometimes, but only after women are deeply involved in deviant street networks. Even then incarceration does not seem to have as much of an impact as one might expect. This observation, of course, may be colored by my sampling technique. Women who were forced out of street life by the action of the criminal justice system would not have been interviewed. For those interviewed, however, contact with the criminal justice system was an occupational hazard; it might affect the nature and conditions of illegal work, but it certainly did not bring that work to a halt or lead women to question their ability to engage in it successfully.

Although the women interviewed might quibble about details of their crimes, arrests, or sentences, they rarely denied committing the crimes of which they were accused. Nor did they object, in principle, to being punished for those crimes. They would very often repeat the rhyme: "I did the crime; I'll do the time." What they did object to was the unpredictability of criminal justice reactions to their acts and, thus, to inconsistencies and inequities in the application of the law. In other words, their objections were directed almost exclusively at those aspects of contacts with the criminal justice system that interfered with their work or relationships in ways which they could not anticipate and that were inconsistent with their past experiences. It was as if they expected the same sorts of responses to their actions no matter how often they were repeated. In some cases this even seemed to be true when the most recent crime committed was a good deal more serious than those committed in the past. They were also very cynical about the standards used to mete out justice to different categories of people and about the arbitrariness with which such laws were enforced and sentences arrived at. They were often outraged by the morally superior stands of the judges who handled their cases, and especially of the police officers who arrested them. Their contacts with the criminal justice system fostered neither respect nor fear, but quite often, rather, indignation, anger, and disdain. Anita said:

> Serious. Let me tell you. I was a baby when all this happened to me. It was real freaky . . . 'cause all of this stuff, you know, everything I ever got into, no matter what it was or how bad it was, my friends or my "man" could get me out of it. And when this happened to me [a conviction for armed robbery], I couldn't accept it. I escaped. I stayed gone a year

and then I went back and turned myself in. Because I felt like they just put me at the wall, away from everything that I loved and cared about . . . they just put me in prison, you know. I about died when they sended me . . . to me that was just too . . . that was . . . that was just spiteful, you know. It was just low. I mean, ooh, I couldn't see it. And I kept asking, you know, I said, now, how come this happened to me? I said, there's peoples out there doin' everythin'; they're killin' peoples, you know, doin' things. I mean they're doin' everythin' and gettin' away with it. There's peoples out there that hurt children, young children, that get teenagers hooked on drugs and shit. They're out there on the streets. And they take me. I made one mistake, now, since I been grown, all of them other things was from the time I was fifteen up to seventeen, you know. Okay, I did . . . this here is the only case I done since I been grown, and they took my freedom away from me. And they brought all that other, all that I did when I was a teenager up to now, when I was twenty. And I couldn't see . . . I couldn't understand why they were doing that now. I couldn't accept it. Why me? I couldn't accept it.

The perception of an unjust and unpredictable criminal justice system had the curious effect of making the majority of the women feel that the moral world was somehow out of balance and that they were "owed" some illegal acts without punishment as a result. Rosemary summed this up:

I don't think that because I've been in jail, it's gonna stop me from doin' what I do. It just gives me time to sit up and say, well, if you don't do it this way, do it that way, so you don't have to worry about being caught. And, so, that's what I do, sit and think what's the best way I should do things so that I won't have to worry about the police and I know who's who and I won't have to worry about that. They say to me, you can't have no more of this money. You have to stay there. So I feel I have to be paid back, get what's dued me. Somebody owe me!

The world view that emerges with involvement in deviant street networks gives some indication of just how self-contained the world of the female street hustler is. It is very much a world segregated from the world of straight work and square people. The identities characteristic of the women that people this world are also to a certain degree encapsulated by it for the raw materials out of which such identities can be constructed are really not very varied.

CHAPTER
VII

Thoughts on the Underclass, the Women's Movement, and Increases in the Criminality of Women

I began this book by highlighting as dramatically as I could why I thought that theories that linked recent increases in property crimes by women to the most recent wave of the women's movement were substantially incorrect. I suggested that rather than being motivated by the norms and values propounded by organizations like NOW, the women responsible for the observed increases were much more likely to have been motivated directly and indirectly by conditions of poverty and the structures and cultures that emerge out of poverty.

At the outset I also issued a caveat about the relationship between the work at hand, which attempts to detail the lives of female street hustlers, a group of women who are involved in the types of crimes that are on the rise, and theories that attempt to link increases in property crime by women to the women's movement. As I stated there, although dissatisfaction with such theories motivated my study, the study itself in no way tests those theories. What it does do with regard to them is suggestive at best, but suggestive in a way that I think is very important. It paints a picture of a world that is in no way comprehended by those theo-

171

ries and that, indeed, flies in the face of them. That is, I see this study as posing a serious challenge to theories such as Adler's and Simon's. It also suggests a theoretical conception of the entire problem that is quite different from that posed thus far and several derivative explanatory frameworks of a more macro-level sort that might be worth elaboration and testing.

In this regard, the fact that is perhaps most important as a point of departure, a fact that was ignored by Adler (1975) and I think misinterpreted by Simon (1975), is that the increase in the criminality of women has been almost exclusively in the area of *property crimes*. This fact, coupled with a fact that was actually made much of by Simon, the dramatic increase in women's labor force participation that occurred about the same time as the observed increase in female property crimes, leads me to speculate, as did Simon, that there is a relationship there, but one quite different from the one she posed. Generally speaking, it leads me to an examination of the socio-economic factors that have left underclass women and the households they often head in greater need over the last two decades than in the immediately preceding period. Furthermore, in the light of research that suggests a correlation between the property crime rate of women and certain major jolts to the economy that we know had important consequences for women's labor force participation, it suggests an examination of the historical relationship between aggregate changes in women's labor force participation and their criminality.[1]

Thus far there has been little work in this area for several reasons. One is that studies of the relationship between gross indicators of economic health or morbidity such as annual gross national product and/or unemployment rates and property crime rates have proved unenlightening. There are those who would seek to dismiss any relationship between the two out of hand. For example, conservatives, such as James Q. Wilson, have been quick to point out that there is a sense in which (at least on its

---

1. Pollak's 1950 classic, *The Criminality of Women*, makes note of the apparent effect of depression and war on the property crime rate for women, for example. Another investigation is the analysis by Giordano, Kerbel, and Dudley (1981) of the relationship between the kind and amount of crime committed by women and fluctuations in the economy from 1890 to 1975 as they affected Toledo, Ohio.

face) a major paradox of the 1960s is the situation of "crime amidst plenty" (1975: 3-22). Recent data indicate, however, that the situation of plenty was but an illusion for many Americans and that the situation of women relative to men and blacks relative to whites, for example, did not improve during the 1960s. Perhaps attempts to relate gross economic trends and crime trends

TABLE 4
Unemployment Rates by Sex, 1947-1973

Year	Total	Male	Female	D=M−F	R=M/F
1947	3.9	4.0	3.8	+0.2	1.05
1948	3.8	3.6	4.1	−0.5	0.88
1949	5.9	5.9	6.0	−0.1	0.98
1950	5.3	5.1	5.8	−0.7	0.88
1951	3.3	2.9	4.4	−1.5	0.66
1952	3.1	2.8	3.7	−0.9	0.76
1953	2.9	2.8	3.3	−0.5	0.85
1954	5.6	5.3	6.1	−0.8	0.87
1955	4.4	4.2	4.9	−0.7	0.86
1956	4.2	3.8	4.9	−1.1	0.78
1957	4.3	4.1	4.7	−0.6	0.87
1958	6.8	6.8	6.8	0.0	1.00
1959	5.5	5.3	5.9	−0.6	0.90
1960	5.6	5.4	5.9	−0.5	0.92
1961	6.7	6.5	7.2	−0.7	0.90
1962	5.6	5.3	6.2	−0.9	0.85
1963	5.7	5.3	6.5	−1.2	0.82
1964	5.2	4.7	6.2	−1.5	0.76
1965	4.6	4.0	5.5	−1.5	0.73
1966	3.9	3.3	4.9	−1.6	0.67
1967	3.8	3.1	5.2	−2.1	0.60
1968	3.6	2.9	4.8	−1.9	0.60
1969	3.5	2.8	4.7	−1.9	0.60
1970	4.9	4.4	5.9	−1.5	0.75
1971	5.9	5.3	6.9	−1.6	0.77
1972	5.6	4.9	6.6	−1.7	0.74
1973	4.9	4.1	6.0	−1.9	0.68

SOURCE: "Manpower Report of the President" (Washington, D.C.: GPO, March 1974), Table A-1, p. 253, as cited in Niemi and Lloyd (1975: 199).

err in that they fail to recognize the fact that labor market segmentation might constitute an important intervening variable.

Since the pioneering work of Edna Bonacich (1972), several social scientists have attempted to use dual labor market theory to illuminate the situations of both minority workers and women workers. Following her lead, for example, Beth Niemi and Cynthia Lloyd (1975) addressed themselves to two related aspects of the current observed earnings gap between men and women: first, the fact that the unemployment rate of women has consistently been higher than that of men and, second, the fact that the general trend seems to be a widening of this gap, at the same time that the female labor force participation rate has been rising. Table 4 reflects these trends, and in the light of the discussion in Chapter I of recent increases in female property crimes beginning in the mid to late sixties, reveals an interesting and perhaps significant fact: that was exactly the time when the unemployment rate for women at least relative to men was highest.[2] Niemi and Lloyd use their data to support the "overcrowding" hypothesis as at least a partial explanation of the earnings gap. The overcrowding hypothesis points out that women have been and continue to be largely segregated in certain clerical and service occupations. The occupational segregation of women and men in our economy is certainly substantial and means that, when labor force participation rises, it both depresses the wages of women relative to men and raises their unemployment rate.[3] One might hypothesize that it is precisely these unemployed women who are committing the property crimes discussed above. Alternatively, this group of women whose unemployment is formally recorded

2. One might speculate that this relative difference was related to the fact that, as Willis (1975) shows, more poor men (who would be marginally attached to the labor force in any case) than men who were relatively well off were killed during the Vietnam War, and that the time period at issue here coincides with the height of the killing. These men would have been in the age category which would have made them precisely the men upon whom the women in question were likely to be, at least to some degree, economically dependent.

3. For example, in 1960, 47 percent of all women workers were employed in occupations in which at least 80 percent of the workers in the occupation were female, while only 3 percent of employed men were in these same occupations. On the other hand, only 20 percent of employed women were in occupations in which they represented less than 33 percent of total employment, while almost 90 percent of employed men were in these occupations (Niemi and Lloyd 1975: 198).

may simply signal the existence of another group of women in even more dire circumstances, women who have no attachment to the labor force at all. If the American labor market is segmented by sex, it is also segmented by race/ethnicity. Thus, it is important to note that the women who entered the labor force in large number in the 1960s were, for the most part, women who had not traditionally worked, older white women with children.[4] Does their entry into the labor force disadvantage in any way less-educated, minority women already in the labor force or desirous of entering the labor force. My hunch is that it does. Moreover, this occurred at a time when those jobs that were often the lot of this group, jobs such as farm laborer and domestic, were becoming more and more scarce.

This explanation is offered as but an example of the type of theorizing possible once socio-economic factors are introduced with a bit more complexity than they have been in the past. The research agenda suggested here is much broader in scope than the explanation sketched above might indicate, however. Other pressing questions come immediately to mind. Why do both the labor force participation rate and the female property crime rate seem to increase universally (if they indeed do) with the advance of capitalism? Is it, as Albert Szymanski suggests (1976: 38), that the motive for capital to draw women into the labor force springs not only from the profitability of their labor but also from the fact that the entry of women into the wage labor force allows capital to increase the rate of exploitation of *male* workers, not because they necessarily compete in the same market but because men no longer have to be paid enough to support themselves *and* those women dependent on them? This might explain the fact that it is married women with children who were drawn disproportionately into the labor force in the 1960s. But what about single mothers? The fact that mothers in general have a higher rate of labor force participation than non-mothers speaks at least in part to the motive driving women into the labor force. It would appear to be economic necessity along with the increasing demand of capital for cheap labor. It is interesting to note in this regard that

4. If work outside the home were a good measure of "liberation," then it would be proper to say that black women, in particular, have always been liberated, since they have always worked outside the home in large numbers.

56 percent of all females in American prisons in recent years were the sole support of their children. A third of these had one minor child at home, 20 percent had two children, and another 23 percent had three or more (U.S. General Accounting Office 1979: 10).

Having speculated a bit on the situation of female labor force participation during times of general economic expansion, such as the wartime 1960s were, when it has been suggested that women's property crime rate increases, let me speculate briefly on the situation of economic crisis.[5] Otto Pollak (1950) observes that during depressions the property crime rate for women falls (155). Ruth Milkman (1976), in criticizing the widely accepted notion that women form a "reserve army" that is integrated into the labor market during periods of expansion and expelled with contractions, argues that, while economic expansion draws women into the labor force, at least during the depression of 1929 the sexual segregation of occupations created an inflexibility in the labor market that prevented their expulsion during the crisis of contraction. Women's unpaid household work was the arena, she argues, where they were forced to "take up the slack" in the economy during the crisis (72–79). There might be a sense, then, in which women may be "overemployed" during times of economic crisis, thus accounting for their lowered property crime rates. This would lead one to posit at least a slowing of the increases in property crime rates for women during times of recession.

But it is possible that here, too, there might be a differential impact on women by social class and/or race/ethnicity? At this point we have no way of knowing. However, in an analysis of the economics of female criminality that employs data from Toledo, Ohio, police blotters for the years 1890 to 1976, Peggy Giordano, Sandra Kerbel, and Sandra Dudley (1981) note that the depression year that is part of their study, 1930, shows *significant increases* in crimes committed by women, particularly in the areas of robbery, burglary, theft, and embezzlement. They note that an examination of the depression years suggests that, like more recent labor market shifts, the increase that occurred during the depression was due primarily to the entry into the market of married women

---

5. See Steffensmeier, Rosenthal, and Shehan (1980) for a treatment of the property crime rates of women during a time of economic expansion at variance with Pollak's view presented here.

whose motivation was family economic survival. They argue that this pattern had the effect of placing single women in an even more precarious economic position than they were in at the time simply by virtue of their singleness. It seems that during the depression, WPA work was differentially awarded the married of both sexes. They feel that it is reasonable to hypothesize that at least some of these single women (and men) included criminality in the range of adaptations they developed for surviving. As a result, they conclude:

> We thus see it as significant that the major, consistent increases have been documented in the area of property crimes. With Simon we would highlight the importance of the greater labor-force participation of women. However, this analysis of offense types as well as the characteristics of women arrested suggests that the increases may reflect the fact that certain categories of women (e.g., young, single, minority) are now in an even more unfavorable position in the labor market at the same time that they are increasingly expected to function independently (81).

But let's travel from the macro level to more micro considerations. The description of the social organization of the criminal activities that comprise street hustling contained in this book also suggest another complicating factor. How are the crime rates of females related to those of males? The research reported here implies that one cannot explain the pattern of female criminal activity, at least as it is engaged in by female street hustlers, while ignoring the criminal behavior of the men for and with whom they work. Just how both the male and female crime *rates* and the *patterns* of criminal behaviors for men and women are interrelated, however, is unclear. The findings presented in the preceding chapter do seem to suggest that they are related in ways that are very significant. Specifically, they suggest that for every "man" there is likely to be more than one "woman" and that "men" may, at times, be able to engage in crime with a certain impunity because they benefit from the illegal work of their "women." Moreover, it is quite likely that this occurs at a predictable time in their criminal careers.

It is clear that not all male criminals are equally likely to become "men." The ones I heard about were overwhelmingly black men with lengthy criminal records who were in their late twenties and older and were often addicted to heroin or cocaine. Just how males are recruited to be "men" is also unclear. However, the findings discussed in this work do point to a clear relationship between the criminality of a particular cohort of men and a particular cohort of women that warrants further research. They suggest that there may be a certain lag between increases in the rates for a particular group of males and parallel increases for a particular group of females as well as changes in the patterning of criminal action by sex cohort. Specifically, the fact that males who have already passed their peak periods of criminal activity may be at least partially responsible for future rashes of criminal activity among women whom they control implies that, were the needed data available, statistical analysis might reveal interesting cohort effects for delimited geographical areas of the sort described here.

One might hypothesize from the findings presented here that a particular cohort of men that have come to a point at which their criminal behavior begins to result in diminishing rewards because of the increasing costs of contacts with the criminal justice system may become at least part of the impetus that leads to the initiation of a related cohort of young women into street life who, over the next ten or fifteen years, will be responsible for increasingly serious street crimes themselves. This model is, of course, complicated by the fact that there is some interaction among the two cohorts with regard to criminal activity and that female street hustlers themselves may initiate young women into "the life." It would be interesting to see if a quantitative study could reveal the general pattern that is suggested by this qualitative one, however.

An additional complication for study would be an attempt to investigate the relationship just described against the backdrop of the distribution of familial form in a particular geographic area for, if "men" provide the pull that attracts women to the street life, it appears to be a complex of familial variables that provides the push or is effective in counteracting the pull. In addition, a quality ethnographic study of street "men" might further complicate the theoretical model posed as well as yield findings about the nature and functioning of deviant street net-

works complementary to, and perhaps corrective of, those presented here that would be significant in and of themselves.

In a different but related sphere, if the insights recorded in
this work concerning the significance of the intersection of familial and deviant networks for the recruitment of young women to
street life are accurate, then examinations of those economic and
social conditions that foster the development of familial networks
also warrant further study with reference to their possible influence on the criminal behavior of women and perhaps men, as
well. Such studies offer methodological challenges that may well
be insurmountable. However, suggestive quantitative studies of
the relationship between familial forms among low-income
blacks, whites, and Hispanics and overall household income have
already begun to yield analyses supportive of some of the findings
reported here.

Recent work by Ronald Angel and Marta Tienda (1982), for
example, examines the relationship between household composition and sources of household income among these three groups
in order to determine the extent to which extended living arrangements help buffer the effects of labor market disadvantages
faced by minority household heads. Results of logit and
regression analyses indicate that differences in the prevalence of
extended family households reflect the primarily group-specific
differences in the propensity to extend, but that this demographic
mechanism may also serve as a compensatory strategy for sup-
plementing the temporarily or chronically low earnings of
minority household heads. In black and Hispanic households,
non-nuclear members were found to contribute significantly to
total household income. Non-nuclear members in white households appeared not to participate significantly in the generation
of household income. What Angel and Tienda looked at, however, was household (of co-residing individuals) income as
recorded in the 1976 Survey of Income and Education. Although
their conclusions support the findings in this work in that they
suggest differences in the propensity to extend in response to
market conditions and for cultural reasons between black and
Hispanic households, on the one hand, and white households, on
the other, that I would then argue have an impact of the recruitment of young women from these groups to deviant street networks, the qualitative findings described here also suggest that

there may be significant differences between Hispanics and blacks with regard to familial form that may affect the criminality of young females from either group. This difference and its significance for our purposes may be obscured by the unit of analysis employed by Angel and Tienda. They themselves point out that their

> analysis is based on the *extended family household* and not the *extended* family. In common usage, the latter refers to interaction patterns among related individuals, whereas the former refers more specifically to the actual living arrangements of relatives. While both types are pertinent to the investigation of economic interactions among relatives, an analysis of the monetary exchanges based on co-residence patterns tells only part of the story. Informal exchange activities among households are not outmoded forms of social organization in the process of extinction. This study has provided an empirical basis for the claim that families rely on immediate relatives or non-nuclear members within the household for support when social and economic demands are great. But assistance need not be economic to render economic benefit. Troll (1971, p. 265) has identified four aspects of kinship exchange: (1) residential propinquity; (2) type and frequency of interaction; (3) economic interdependence or mutual aid; and (4) varied qualitative measures of familism, value transmission, and affectional bonds. Each of these has potential for clarifying how formal and informal exchanges take place within and *between* households (p. 1380) [emphasis mine].

There are several points that need to be made here with regard to the present study. First, as Angel and Tienda point out, both non-monetary and *inter*-household exchange is important in assessing income equity and economic coping strategies. Stack's (1974) research and that presented here suggest that for low-income blacks the domestic network, by its very nature a much less easily delimited unit, may be a more appropriate unit of analysis than the family, however defined, or the household (of co-residing individuals). Although efforts to create concepts that differentiate the "extended family" as an economic unit (which I believe is characteristic of low-income Hispanics) from the "domestic network" (which I would hypothesize is more characteristic of low-income blacks) and reflect the degree to which these two sorts of familial forms overlap (as I believe they do) may be fraught with difficulty, they are likely to yield a much better understanding of how different groups cope with economic stress and how these coping strategies may relate to other social problems typical of the groups in question.

Second, we need to find a way to estimate the degree to which such familial forms may be correlated with opportunities for the group, despite the moral scruples of some of its members, to benefit from illegal work. Angel and Tienda point out that their analysis ignores non-monetary exchanges. It also ignores, as does most research of this sort, income derived directly and indirectly from illegal work (as does the ethnographic work of Stack and Valentine). Lastly, it is important that we try to answer the following question: To what degree do the familial forms that emerge as a response to particular sorts of economic stress and that become embedded in a group's culture simultaneously allow the group to cope in some measure with that economic stress and make that group more vulnerable to a plethora of other social problems, of which the recruitment of the young to deviant street networks is but one?[6]

Longitudinal studies that attempt to relate market conditions to familial forms or familial forms to patterns of illegal work would only yield some of the answers to the puzzle posed for one interested in how these particular social phenomena interrelate. The relationship between female criminality and opportunities for legitimate work that might compete with opportunities for illegal work also needs to be studied as do the attitudes and values that color the perceptions of underclass adolescents with regard to both the legitimate and the illegitimate opportunities structures. Studies of the political economy of women's labor force participation in illegal work might also go far in shedding

6. Another social problem that I have argued is antecedent and contributory to recruitment to street hustling for young women is their early entry into adult status via motherhood. Hogan and Kitagawa (1985) have recently identified family structure as an important variable that is independently predictive of early pregnancy itself as well.

light on some of the issues raised by this research. All of these musings are highly speculative but, I hope, suggestive of the sorts of research problems that might be generated if this line of inquiry were taken seriously. The methodological impediments to undertaking such research are not negligible, but neither are they completely insurmountable. The questions beg for answers; the terrain is largely uncharted; the task lies before us.

Afterword on the Research Experience

I was living in Chicago when I first became interested in the area of women and crime generally, and in the Adler/Simon thesis about the relationship between women's liberation and increases in women's property crime rates in particular. I was working part-time in a downtown Chicago bar disturbingly called the Meet Market. It was there that I first came upon female street hustlers. I had never met such women before. My first thought was that, if these were the women whose behavior accounted for the observed increases, then the Adler/Simon thesis was surely in error. This led me to begin to go to Women's Court in Chicago (commonly known as Hooker's Court) to try to determine a bit more about what these women did and how the courts reacted to their behavior.

When I came to Milwaukee to teach, it was with these experiences at the back of my mind and a very strong feeling that a *qualitative* study of female offenders would add much to our general knowledge of women and crime. Such a study might even shed some light on the issues raised by Adler and Simon that so intrigued me.

I got permission from Wisconsin Correctional Services to interview at the House of Correction almost immediately. Horizon House and Arc House were also easily accessed. The Wisconsin Department of Corrections gave me permission to interview at both Taycheedah Correctional Institution (the state penal facility for women offenders) upstate and Metro Center, an arm of Taycheedah in downtown Milwaukee that houses women soon to be released from Taycheedah—on the condition that the heads of each of those institutions did not object. The warden at Taycheedah denied me access, while the director of Metro Center was very willing to cooperate. I started interviewing in the spring of 1979 and was involved in gathering data pretty much full-time for the next six months.

I remember very well my first visit to Horizon House. I had been invited to dinner, after which I was to describe my study and recruit informants. I thought it best to dress casually. I wore jeans and a T-shirt and sneakers. I wanted to minimize the difference between myself and the women I was trying to get to know. I am a tiny blondish woman with a pronounced Boston accent.

I drove to Horizon House in the heart of Milwaukee's center city. Especially given that I was not terribly familiar with the layout of the city, I found the depressed nature of the neighborhoods I was driving through a bit intimidating. I had lived on the Southside of Chicago for seven years, so I wasn't seeing anything I hadn't seen before, but the fact that I was unfamiliar with the area coupled with its poverty and the fact that I was launching a new study likewise in uncharted territory all served to make me uneasy. A staff person welcomed me cordially when I arrived and then exited for the day. Dinner was being served, so I sat down. There were, perhaps, eight others seated as well, mostly black women. A radio blared Donna Summer's "Bad Girls." I thought: "How ironic!" One attractive black woman danced over to the table and was seated. She was the last, and people began to pass the food. I was pretty much ignored, although people did see to it that I received a hearty portion of a wonderful meal. I later discovered that I wasn't really being ignored. The women thought I was a new Horizon House resident, and the norm is that one respects a new resident's privacy as much as possible upon her arrival. People are helpful when approached, but feel that they have no right to intrude upon another's probable pain. One would especially never ask a new arrival about the events that surrounded her coming to Horizon House. In any event, current residents realize that they will learn about the new person soon enough in the context of group therapy.

Knowing none of this at the time, I was very uncomfortable,

however, and decided to just sit and eat and take in as much as I could. People talked and joked and, occasionally, sang along with the radio. I couldn't understand half of what was being said. With a sinking feeling, I started to question whether or not I could ever be comfortable enough personnally to do this study. What would happen when I began to interview women on their own turf, outside the safety of a homey halfway house or the relative security of a jail?

After dinner, the women cleared the table and washed the dishes. Not really knowing what I was supposed to do, I silently helped. Then, most of them returned to the living room. By that time, the night staffperson had arrived. She interrupted the animated conversation that was being engaged in by several of the women and introduced me. As I addressed the group, a few women continued to talk. One stared out the window. Another said flatly, "Do we have to stay here?" The remaining women listened with varying levels of interest.

I explained that I was writing a book about women like them. I noted, furthermore, that I hoped that the book would make people more sympathetic to their lives and to the situations of their children. I told the women that I wanted to do life history interviews, that the interviews would be tape-recorded, and that their anonymity would be protected. I admitted my ignorance of their world and told them that they had a lot they could teach me. Last, I offered a ten-dollar remuneration for each interview. The offer of money did it. I had volunteers aplenty.

The next evening, I began to interview. I completed five intensive life histories over the next several days. I was much more at ease one on one and had little difficulty dealing with the rhythms of Black English in that context. It was only later that I became aware that my informants were accommodating me with their version of White English. I did have problems with the meanings of particular words and phrases. Although I had admitted my ignorance of their world, I didn't want to appear too square. As a result, when I couldn't determine the meaning of a word or phrase from the context in which it was used, I felt comfortable asking for one or two definitions. Beyond that, I would save my questions about terminology for another time or another informant. Thus if I had already asked a woman to explain to me what a Jones was (physical manifestations of drug dependency) or what wives-in-law were (women who worked for the same man), I might save further questions of this sort for someone else.

There was also the problem of not knowing when women were not being completely truthful or when they were, in fact, lying. My fear at the outset was that this would be a major problem. That fear was almost immediately allayed, however, by what I felt was often an almost complete lack of reticence among the women I spoke with. I later concluded that, in these first interviews, the women were very candid about some things that I would, perhaps, not have been as open about—for example, their criminal activity—and less frank about things that I would have been more open about—for example, personal relationships. I learned that one needed to probe more when asking questions about these latter areas. Later, that was less necessary.

After I had been in the field for a while, several things happened that I think improved both the quality and the quantity of the data gathered during the interviews. In addition to becoming more aware of the vocabulary of the streets, I had become better acquainted with the subject areas that might elicit seminal information. Also, I came to have a certain reputation among at least some networks of female street hustlers. At the end of the interviewing period, women would say: "Oh, yeah, you're the professor doing the book." Women also became curious about my age, my personal life, and whether or not I had ever lived the fast life myself. Thus, any fears they had about my being a vice officer or narcotics agent in disguise were put to rest and some women actually wanted "to be in the book."

Having completed the first round of interviews at Horizon House, I went to interview at the House of Correction in Franklin, Wisconsin, a good forty-minute drive south of Milwaukee. This was a "real" penal institution with huge locked doors, guards, uniforms, barbed wire, etc. The women there are housed in one large, locked dormitory. Initially I addressed the women there as a group about who I was and what I was doing. There were women who were at work in Milwaukee on work release when this occurred, however, so on subsequent days when I came to interview my mission was explained by a drug counselor from Wisconsin Correctional Services. Women who were interested in being interviewed were brought to me one by one in the chapel.

For many reasons, getting the group together so that I might address them was simply not a realistic thing to attempt day after day.

Thus, I was not able to control as much as I would have liked just which women I interviewed at the House of Correction. Two women were brought to me who were clearly mentally defective, for example. They were very anxious to receive the ten-dollar remuneration, however, and I felt I had, in conscience, to interview them and award them the subject fee. This I did, but the interview data were truly useless.

Not only was the mental state of the informant not subject to my control, but the quality of the tape recordings themselves were often problematic there. Generally speaking, there is a level of activity and crowding there that simply made quiet, private interviewing difficult to achieve. For example, on several occasions male inmates wandered into the chapel during the interviews to investigate what was going on, in search of company, and clearly in search of possible sex. I found these interruptions annoying and, at least initially, rather frightening. This was especially true on one occasion when I was alone in the chapel and a male inmate strolled in. I had the real sense, as I had not on other similar occasions, that during our conversation about who I was and what I was doing he was calculating the risks and benefits associated with sexually molesting me. The female inmate I was to interview entered the room just about then and quickly chased him from it in the best Black English falsetto harangue I had heard in some time. She comprehended the whole situation in an instant and acted in a sort of offhand, but commanding way. I flashed her a grateful smile and tried to appear as if I took it all in stride.

I also recall one evening when a severe thunderstorm raged outside and the lights kept flickering and threatening to go out. I was very uneasy, especially given the absence of the usual bevy of daytime workers. Indeed, the fact that this was clearly an institution for men was almost continually problematic. I recall feeling terribly frustrated one afternoon when I was attempting to record interviews above the din rising from a particularly noisy basketball game being played in the courtyard where the men often exercised.

It was while at the House of Correction that I attempted to

expand my sample to include non-institutionalized female street
hustlers. I asked women to call similarly engaged women on the
outside, explain what I was doing, and make arrangements for me
to make contact. These calls began to pan out and I, simultaneously, started to interview at Metro Center.

At least six weeks had intervened since that unsettling
dinner at Horizon House. I felt that I had the vocabulary down
and had begun to refine my interview questions in response to my
increasing knowledge and in an attempt to search for evidence
that would disprove some hypotheses I was beginning to develop
about different facets of the lives and work of female street
hustlers. After achieving a modicum of ease and self-confidence
when interacting with these women one on one, the idea that I
would now be less able to control the turf upon which the conversations occurred once again raised my anxiety level. I was so
intrigued with what I was learning and had become so convinced
of its import that I was not about to give up at that point, however, nor was I going to change my plans to interview women
who were not in some measure captives of the state. I needed to see
whether or not their stories would differ in any significant way
from the stories I had been hearing thus far.

The interviewing at Metro Center was largely uneventful.
The conditions under which the interviewing was done were
neither noisy nor threatening. The women were different from
the generally younger, less crime-involved women I had interviewed up to this point, women who, by and large, had not experienced the isolation and loneliness of the more secure Taycheedah. This was my impression on a gut level; I had to figure out
whether this impression had any basis in reality.

The first non-institutionalized woman I spoke with was
interviewed at her flat. Several other female street hustlers were
there as it was early afternoon and most of them had slept late and
were planning to hustle in the evening. They were smoking marijuana and wandering in and out of the living room in which the
interview was taking place. We eventually moved to a bedroom
for more privacy. After the interview, I spoke with several of the
other women and watched "General Hospital" on television. I
could understand what was being said most of the time now and
found myself more frequently switching into Black English during conversations.

A young black male drove up on a motorcycle while we were watching television. He had a woman with a bruised face riding with him. Glancing at her, he made it plain that I was only there because it had been cleared with him and that I was no longer welcome. I felt physically threatened by him and decided that, in the future, I would stay out of the way of the "men" who managed these women as much as possible. From then on, I tried to arrange such interviews on more neutral ground: in Dunkin' Donuts or in the public library downtown or in the home where a woman's child was cared for. This latter site turned out to have numerous advantages because I could sometimes meet and speak with the mothers and siblings of these women.

I've mentioned being afraid, intimidated, and uncomfortable while doing this research. There are several important emotions that I have not mentioned. Especially if I had interviewed at the House of Correction or (on the second or third round) at a halfway house in the evening and had a bit of a drive home, I found that the details of these women's lives would run together in my mind and make me angry, generally upset, and depressed. I was angry that children could grow up in situations like many of these women described growing up in. I was angry that people could so brutalize one another, that they could treat one another as commodities. I was depressed about the lack of realistic options for these women, about the probable futures of their children. I was upset that a society existed that bred so much hatred, discrimination, and inequality. For reasons I do not know, these emotions, as paralyzing as they could have been, were rather motivating forces with regard to the research. In short, because the whole scene became more familiar and because I deliberately set parameters with regard to my contacts with "men" (in my opinion, the only real threats to my safety), and because I learned to communicate in a variant of Black English (the language of the street for female street hustlers regardless of race/ethnicity), the fieldwork for this study became more compelling, interesting, and comfortable as time went on. Perhaps one of the best indicators of this was the fact that dinners at Horizon House were now quite a bit of fun. I joined in the teasing banter that characterizes dinnertime there and actually became the butt of some ribbing myself. And the food was just as good as ever.

There were only two instances where I felt I was injured or

truly at risk while doing the interviewing. One night, the tires on my car were slashed—presumably by a pimp—while I was interviewing in the center city. This left me rather inconvenienced with regard to transport home and, more significantly, somewhat confused and frightened that a "man" should think that I was in any way a threat. In any event, whether or not the culprit was a "man," I was not harassed any further. The other occurrence was also more of an inconvenience than a true injury. Several years after the fieldwork for the study was complete, a check was forged on my checking account in a very professional manner. There were several indications that the person who, at least initially, identified my account as one about which there was enough information to engage in such a forgery was one of my informants. Given the extended networks through which such information is often transmitted and the time that had elapsed, however, it is quite likely that she herself was not the forger.

All in all, the experience of doing this kind of research was, and continues to be, a very rewarding one. It is often depressing, but sometimes exhilarating. It is labor-intense, but, to my mind, well worth the effort both personally and intellectually.

References

Adler, Freda. 1975. *Sisters in Crime*. New York: McGraw-Hill.

Angel, Ronald, and Marta Tienda. 1982. "Determinants of Extended Household Structure: Cultural Pattern or Economic Need?" *American Journal of Sociology* 87 (May): 1360–1383.

Auletta, Ken. 1982. *The Underclass*. New York: Random House.

Beverstock, Frances, and Robert F. Stuckert. 1972. "Metropolitan Milwaukee Fact Book: 1970." Milwaukee: Urban Observatory, University of Wisconsin–Milwaukee.

Bonacich, Edna. 1972. "A Theory of Ethnic Antagonism: The Split Labor Market." *American Sociological Review* 37 (October): 547–559.

Bott, Elizabeth. 1971. *Family and Social Network*. New York: Free Press.

Bowker, Lee H. 1978a. *Women, Crime, and the Criminal Justice System*. Lexington, Mass.: Lexington Books.

———. 1978b. "Women and Drugs: Beyond the Hippie Subculture." Pp. 57–59 in *Women, Crime, and the Criminal Justice System*. Edited by Lee H. Bowker. Lexington, Mass.: Lexington Books.

Brennan, Tim. 1980. "Mapping the Diversity of Runaways: A Descriptive Multivariate Analysis of Selected Social Psychological Background Conditions." *Journal of Family Issues* 1 (June): 189–209.

Brennan, Tim, David Huizinga, and Delbert S. Elliott. 1978. *The Social Psychology of Runaways*. Lexington, Mass.: Lexington Books.

Butler, Dodie, Joe Reinier, and Bill Treanor. 1974. *Runaway House: A Youth-Run Project*. Washington, D.C.: GPO.

ch, Stephen C., and Peggy C. Giordano. 1979. "A Comparative
alysis of Male and Female Delinquency." *The Sociological
Quarterly* 20 (Winter): 131-145.

man, Jane Roberts. 1980. *Economic Realities and the Female
Offender.* Lexington, Mass.: Lexington Books.

ianciara, Jacek. 1978. "Estimation of Industrial Output and Employment: A Progress Report." Pp. 44-59 in *Milwaukee Economy:
Market Forces, Community Problems and Federal Policies.* Edited
by John P. Blair and Ronald S. Edari. Chicago: Federal Reserve
Bank of Chicago.

Cohen, Bernard. 1980. *Deviant Street Networks: Prostitution in New
York.* Lexington, Mass.: Lexington Books.

Edari, Ronald S. 1978. "The Structure of Racial Inequality in the Mil-
waukee Area." Pp. 86-111 in *Milwaukee Economy: Market Forces,
Community Problems and Federal Policies.* Edited by John P.
Blair and Ronald S. Edari. Chicago: Federal Reserve Bank of
Chicago.

Gans, Herbert J. 1962. *The Urban Villagers: Group and Class in the Life
of Italian Americans.* New York: Free Press.

Giordano, Peggy C., Sandra Kerbel, and Sandra Dudley. 1981. "The
Economics of Female Criminality: An Analysis of Police Blotters,
1890-1975." Pp. 65-82 in *Women and Crime in America.* Edited by
Lee H. Bowker. New York: Macmillan.

Gross, Edward. 1968. "Plus Ca Change . . . ? The Sexual Structure of
Occupations over Time." *Social Problems* 16 (Fall): 198-208.

Gurda, John and, Byron Anderson. 1972. *The Near South Side.* Milwaukee: Zion United Church of Christ and Journey House Youth
Center.

Gurin, Patricia. 1985. "Women's Gender Consciousness." *Public Opinion Quarterly* 49 (Summer): 143-163.

Hogan, Dennis P., and Evelyn M. Kitagawa. 1985. "The Impact of Social
Status, Family Structure, and Neighborhoods on the Fertility of
Black Adolescents." *American Journal of Sociology* 90 (January):
825-855.

Howell, Joseph T. 1973. "Selected Socioeconomic Indicators of Milwaukee County, Wisconsin." Milwaukee: Urban Observatory, University of Wisconsin-Milwaukee.

Komarovsky, Mirra. 1967. *Blue-Collar Marriage.* New York: Vintage
Books.

Ladner, Joyce A. 1971. *Tomorrow's Tomorrow: The Black Woman.* New
York: Anchor Books.

LeMasters, Edgar E. 1975. *Blue-Collar Aristocrats.* Madison: University
of Wisconsin Press.

Libertoff, Ken. 1980. "The Runaway Child in America: A Social History." *Journal of Family Issues* 1 (June): 151-164.

Maher, Vanessa. 1976. "Kin, Clients, and Accomplices: Relationships among Women in Morocco." Pp. 52-75 in *Sexual Divisions and Society: Process and Change.* Edited by Diana Leonard Barker and Sheila Allen. London: Tavistock Publications.

Mason, Karen Oppenheim, John L. Czajka, and Sara Arber. 1976. "Change in U.S. Women's Sex-Role Attitudes, 1964-1974." *American Sociological Review* 41 (August): 573-596.

Mata, Alberto G. 1978. "The Drug Street Scene: An Ethnographic Study of Mexican Youth in South Chicago." Ph.D. dissertation, University of Notre Dame, Department of Sociology.

Milkman, Ruth. 1976. "Women's Work and Economic Crisis: Some Lessons of the Great Depression." *Review of Radical Political Economics* 8 (Spring): 73-79.

Miller, Eleanor M. 1983. "A Cross-Cultural Look at Women and Crime: An Essay Review." *Contemporary Crises* 7 (January): 59-70.

Milwaukee Journal. March 27, 1985. "City 1st in Birth to Black Teens." Part 2, pp. 1 and 5.

———. May 26, 1985. "Prostitutes Return Where They're Not Wanted." Part 2, pp. 1 and 4.

Moore, Joan. 1982. Personal communication based on her ongoing research with Chicana addicts.

Morris, Monica B. 1973. "The Public Definition of a Social Movement." *Sociology and Social Research* 57 (July): 526-543.

Mukherjee, Satyanshu K., and R. William Fitzgerald. 1981. "The Myth of Rising Female Crime." Pp. 127-166 in *Women and Crime.* Edited by Satyanshu K. Mukherjee and Jocelynne A. Scutt. Sydney, Austral.: George Allen & Unwin.

Niemi, Beth, and Cynthia Lloyd. 1975. "Sex Differentials in Earnings and Unemployment Rates." *Feminist Studies* 2: 195-200.

Noblit, George W., and Janie W. Burcart. 1976. "Women and Crime: 1960-1970." *Social Science Quarterly* 56 (March): 650-657.

Nye, F. Ivan. 1980. "Runaways: Some Critical Issues for Professionals and Society." Cooperative Extension Bulletin no. 0744. Pullman, Wash.: Washington State University.

Opinion Research Corporation. 1976. *National Statistical Survey of Runaway Youth.* Princeton, N.J.: Opinion Research Corp.

Palay, Miriam G. 1984. "Census Facts: Milwaukee Areas and Neighborhoods, 1970-1980 Statistics Compared." Milwaukee Division of Urban Outreach, University of Wisconsin-Milwaukee and University of Wisconsin-Extension.

Pollak, Otto. 1950. *The Criminality of Women.* Philadelphia: University of Pennsylvania Press.

Robey, Ames. 1969. "The Runaway Girl." Pp. 127–137 in *Family Dynamics and Female Sexual Delinquency*. Edited by Otto Pollak and Alfred S. Friedman. Palo Alto: Science and Behavior Books.

Rosenbaum, Marsha. 1981. "Women Addicts' Experience of the Heroin World." *Urban Life* 10 (April): 65–91.

Rubin, Lillian Breslow. 1976. *Worlds of Pain*. New York: Basic Books.

Simon, Rita James. 1975. *Women and Crime*. Lexington, Mass.: Lexington Books.

———. 1977. "Women and Crime in Israel." Pp. 81–89 in *Criminology in Perspective: Essays in Honor of Israel Drapkin*. Edited by Simka F. Landau and Leslie Sebba. Lexington, Mass.: Lexington Books.

Social Science Research Committee, University of Chicago. 1963. Pp. xiii–xiv of "Local Community Fact Book, Chicago Metropolitan Area, 1960." Mimeo. Chicago: University of Chicago, Department of Sociology.

Stack, Carol B. 1974. *All Our Kin: Strategies for Survival in a Black Community*. New York: Harper Colophon Books.

Steffensmeier, Darrell J. 1980. "Sex Differences in Patterns of Adult Crime, 1965–77: A Review and Assessment." *Social Problems* 58 (June): 1080–1108.

Steffensmeier, Darrell J., and John Kokenda. 1979. "The Views of Contemporary Male Thieves Regarding Patterns of Female Criminality." Paper presented at the annual meetings of the American Society of Criminology, Philadelphia.

Steffensmeier, Darrell J., Alvin S. Rosenthal, and Constance Shehan. 1980. "World War II and Its Effect on the Sex Differential in Arrests: An Empirical Test of the Sex-Role Equality and Crime Proposition." *The Sociological Quarterly* 21 (Summer): 403–416.

Suttles, Gerald D. 1968. *The Social Order of the Slum*. Chicago: University of Chicago Press.

Szymanski, Albert. 1976. "The Socialization of Women's Oppression: A Marxist Theory of the Changing Position of Women in Advanced Capitalist Society." *The Insurgent Sociologist* 16 (Winter): 31–58.

Tien, Yuan, editor. 1962. *Milwaukee Metropolitan Fact Book: 1940, 1950, 1960*. Madison: University of Wisconsin Press.

U.S. Department of Commerce, Bureau of the Census. 1970. *Historical Statistics of the United States, Colonial Times to 1970*. Vol. 1. Washington, D.C.: GAO.

U.S. General Accounting Office. 1979. *Female Offenders: Who Are They and What Are the Problems Confronting Them?* Washington, D.C.: GAO.

Valentine, Bettylou. 1978. *Hustling and Other Hard Work*. New York: Free Press.

Walker, Deborah Klein. 1975. *Runaway Youth: An Annotated Bibliography and Literature Review.* Washington, D.C.: GPO.

Wattenberg, Willian W. 1956. "Boys Who Run Away from Home." *Journal of Education Psychology* 47: 335–343.

Willis, John. 1975. "Variations in State Casualty Rates in World War II and the Vietnam War." *Social Problems* 22 (April): 558–568.

Wilson, James Q. 1975. *Thinking about Crime.* New York: Vintage.

Wisconsin Department of Industry, Labor, and Human Relations. 1979. "Milwaukee SMSA, WOW, and Milwaukee County Annual Planning Information." Mimeo. Milwaukee: Milwaukee Job Service Division.

Index